Cryptozoology

An Armchair Hunter's Basic Guide

Cryptid Sightings, Stories, Evidence,
Hoaxes, and More

By Rex Cutty

Foreword

We go through this every time. I'm not telling you who I am. You don't need to ask anymore. I wouldn't tell you when we were talking zombies. Ditto for vampires. And now?

Dude, seriously, armchair cryptozoology is just one step off an Area 51 convention. This is something I do for *fun*. You know, like passing the time during the apocalypse before Nessie went all mutant, married Godzilla, and they trashed Tokyo?

(That's just a little cryptid humor. Lighten up.)

You don't need my freaking résumé for us to sit down and talk Chupacabras. But fine, I'll give you the basic list of what I'm not. Not SEAL trained. (In my dreams! Those guys are bad ass!) Not SWAT.

And I'm not some big, *bona fide* monster hunter. If you're searching for a read full of personal experiences, this is not the book you're looking for. Move on.

I'm just a dude with a pulse trying to keep it that way. When it comes to cryptids, I like to keep my options open where belief is concerned.

Trust me. The longer you look at these kinds of reports, the better you'll get at spotting the fakers. It's harder in the digital age, but a bad story is still a bad story, no matter how many PhotoShop filters get thrown in the fight.

For the record, I think the fakers are real losers that are making it harder for the people who are serious about cryptozoology to prove that we don't know everything there is to know about our world and we have not identified every living thing on the planet.

I keep up with this stuff because if I ever do flip on the news and the talking head tells me something has coming walking out of the lake or the woods or swooping down from the sky, I want to have a little advance intel – along with all the other "preparatory" stuff back in the dusty corners of the old gray cells.

The Internet has made that kind of information gathering incredibly easy, so I've rounded up more than 30 relevant websites to help you get started with your own reading list and put them at the back of this book.

So, there's all that behind this project, and then there's the fact that I don't sit around waiting on anybody to teach me anything. I get interested in stuff. I work out the basics for myself. Sometimes I sit down and write about said basics in the interest of sharing.

Here's the specific reason why I'm writing about this topic. In 1972 I saw a beyond bad movie called *The Monster of Boggy Creek* that changed my perspective on what constitutes a "monster."

That film, horrible though it was, put cryptozoology on my radar where it's stayed ever since. I'll tell you the whole story in Chapter 1, and I will share my only cryptid sighting — and it's a classic. (Nobody I know really believes me, by the way, and I don't give a rodent's fat furry backside if you do either.)

The main point of this book is just to share some sketches of cryptid critters I've especially enjoyed reading about or following through the years. So crack open a brew and kick back. We're just shooting the bovine by-product here. Nothing more serious than that.

Unless you got Bigfoot standing on your front porch. If that's the case? You're on your own . . . but get pictures.

Acknowledgments

I firmly acknowledge that there are some crazy things in this word. Things we do not discuss and generally fear. Well, I don't live in fear. I survive and can help you survive too!

Table of Contents

Table of Contents

Table of Contents

Table of Contents

Chapter 1 - What is Cryptozoology?

Okay, kiddies. I think we've already established that Uncle Rex is not a spring chicken. A lot of you may remember the first time you saw *Jaws* – TV, DVD, or Blu-Ray.

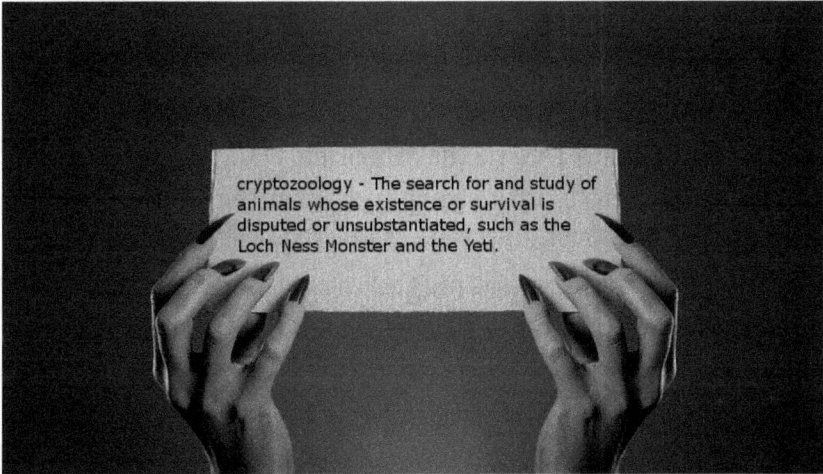

cryptozoology - The search for and study of animals whose existence or survival is disputed or unsubstantiated, such as the Loch Ness Monster and the Yeti.

Me? I was at Danny Fremont's birthday party and he made us all sit on the front row of the dinky little theater in our hometown. The minute that music started, I knew I was in trouble.

That movie – and the idea that something that big could be swimming around in the ocean — scared me enough I almost needed to go home for clean shorts.

Never mind that Benchley later said he was sorry he gave sharks a bad rap. You can go swim with the big sweet toothy minnows if you want to. I'm staying on dry land.

Not that I necessarily think dry land is any safer, but at

least I won't go out whining that all we needed was a bigger boat. But I digress.

Turn the clock back three years from my *Jaws* experience. Same crappy little theater. But this time the movie was *The Legend of Boggy Creek* and it was so much worse than *Jaws* in terms of scaring the bejeebers out of me, I had nightmares for months.

That was 1972 and I've never forgotten walking out of that movie house onto a dark street and sprinting to jump into my Mom's Chevy Malibu before any "thing" lurking in any shadow jumped out and dragged me off. A damned alley cat would have given me a heart attack that night.

When I sat down to start writing this book, I went over to YouTube and watched the *Boggy Creek* trailer. Rated G? Are you freaking kidding me?

Yeah, yeah. The acting was like sub-*Tremors* bad, the "special" effects are ridiculous, and it was nothing but a horror movie trying to pass as a documentary.

But here's the thing that did me in and changed my life when I saw that movie for the first time. I wasn't interested in playing film critic back then. The fact that the movie, bad though it might have been, was based on a true cryptid, pretty much blew me away.

That's why we're starting this discussion with the Fouke Monster, also known as the Southern Sasquatch.

A Word on This Text

Now, let's get one thing straight. This is not one of those books that will claim to offer any evidence for or against the existence of a single critter mentioned in these pages. I don't go running around out there looking for any of these cryptids. This is my armchair hobby.

Cryptozoology is the kind of topic that gets me to stop and watch something when I'm channel surfing. Reading books and articles about the subject and watching documentaries about these "mythic" beasts is fun for me. I thought everybody was interested in the same thing until I had lunch with my buddy Pete a few months back and got his standard, "are you fricking kidding me? line.

Turns out he'd never heard of half of these animals, and even though he was skeptical as hell, we talked about them all afternoon while steadily killing one pot of coffee after another in the little rat trap diner we favor for our more intellectual discussions.

At some point Pete said, "You ought to write this stuff down." I was like, "Pete, man, it's all over the Internet." And he said, "Yeah, but I wouldn't have ever paid any attention to any of it if you hadn't made it sound interesting."

I really don't care what you do to pass your time, but for me, cryptozoology is better than stamp collecting or chainsaw art. Well, okay, I *tried* chainsaw art and just wound up with a lot of sawdust.

Everybody has to have something to do to kick back and this particular hobby is just a shade off conspiracy theories, which I also enjoy. I'm just here to tell some stories and lay out the framework for the "facts" behind some of my favorite cryptids. What you do with it is up to you.

Me? I'm not looking for Bigfoot, but if I run into him, I'll buy him a beer, 'cause that's just how ole Rex rolls.

The Fouke Monster

Now, back to Boggy Creek. From 1971 to 1974 eyewitness reports cropped up describing a seven-foot / 2.13 meters creature living in Miller County in southwestern Arkansas.

(And no, I'm not going to start in with the Arkansas inbreeding jokes. Even I won't go for fruit hanging that low.)

The unidentified animal was seen on Boggy Creek north and east of a tiny town of less than a thousand souls, which bears the unfortunate name "Fouke."

The area is certainly prime country for monster sighting. If you drive through there, you're going to find a lot of flat land crisscrossed with rivers and creeks and covered in dense forests.

You can get lost back in there pretty fast, and if something didn't want to be found, that would be pretty easy to pull off.

Common Factoid: One thing you're going to find that a lot of these cryptid stories have in common is that the creatures live in dense or inaccessible environments.

That can be a deep lake, a swamp, a forest, or a frozen mountaintop. It doesn't really matter. The underlying idea is always the same.

The setting is one that's a good hiding place, adding some creditability to the notion that a big creature could be living close to human habitation and never be spotted.

Some people said they saw the creature running like a monkey and described the beast as having long shaggy hair and a foul odor — kind of like a wet dog that just got sprayed by a very ticked off skunk.

And, of course, the thing had red eyes.

Common Factoid: The more you study cryptozoology, the more red eyes you're going to run into. Get used to it.

Personally, I think a lot of it has to do with flashbulbs and flash lights at night. You know? How Fido or Fluffy go all laser eyes when you take a picture?

I'm almost more shocked to hear a cryptid story that leaves out the red eyes.

Tracks were found in the area around Fouke. Some were said to be 17 inches / 43.18 cm long and 7 inches / 17.78 cm wide with just three toes.

I'm sure you'll be shocked to learn there's a website. Heck, there's a website for everything. At your leisure, trot on over and enjoy The Beast of Boggy Creek at www.foukemonster.net.

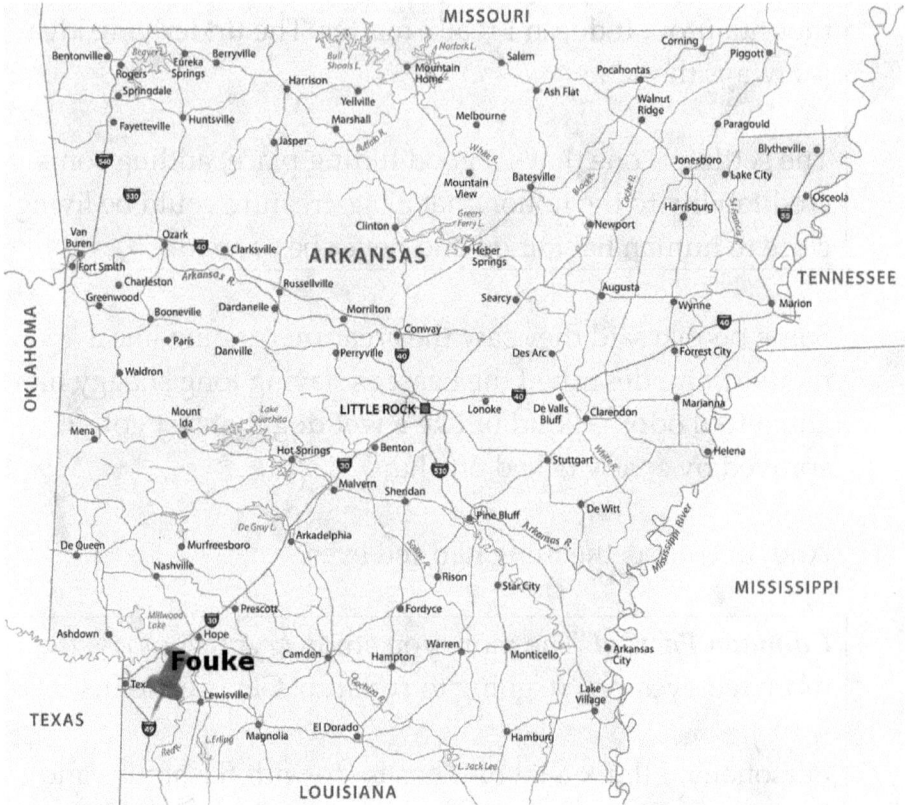

If nothing else, you'll get a kick out of the stills from the movie. Personally, I feel for the actor who must have been dying in that suit.

I especially like the shot of the good ole Arkansas boys in their white Hanes undershirts out on the front porch with a 12-gauge, 'cause there's nothing in the world you can't fix with a 12-gauge and/or duct tape.

(Which actually may be true. See my previous book *Zombie Apocalypse: A Survival Guide.*)

According to the website, "Over the years, the creature has been seen by countless people, including respected citizens, experienced hunters, famous musicians, and even a police officer."

Well, there you go. A famous musician tells me he's seen a seven-foot-tall, hairy creature, I am going to believe him because no musician has ever been under the influence of anything mind altering at any time.

But the Fouke monster didn't just magically appear in the Seventies. The sightings originally began in 1908. Between then and the rash of accounts that inspired the film that scarred me for life, a lot of folks saw the creature, and a goodly number took shots at it.

They all missed, because if you think buck fever will throw your aim off, wait until you get an attack of what-the-hell-is-that ebola. Even with a 12-gauge you're not going to hit much when you're running as fast as you can in the opposite direction.

As for the "musical" connection, that was from a sighting in 1967. Again quoting from FoukeMonster.net:

> "While driving late one night, a teenager (who later became a Grammy-award winning musician) and his cousin see a hair-covered, bipedal creature running along Highway 71. They were residents of

Texarkana and had never heard of the Fouke
Monster or Bigfoot. The teenager didn't realize what
he seen [sic] until years later when he saw *The Legend
of Boggy Creek*."

But here's the account of the story that really touched off
the hysteria in 1971 as it was written by reporter Jim Powell
for the *Texarkana Gazette*:

Elizabeth Ford said she was sleeping in the front
room of the frame house [she and her husband and
another couple were renting] when, "I saw the
curtain moving on the front window and a hand
sticking through the window. At first I thought it
was a bear's paw but it didn't look like that. It had
heavy hair all over it and it had claws. I could see its
eyes. They looked like coals of fire ... real red," she
said. "It didn't make any noise. Except you could
hear it breathing."

Ford said they spotted the creature in back of the
house with the aid of a flashlight. "We shot several
times at it then and then called Ernest Walraven,
constable of Fouke. He brought us another shotgun
and a stronger light. We waited on the porch and
then saw the thing closer to the house. We shot again
and thought we saw it fall. Bobby, Charles and
myself started walking to where we saw it fall," he
said.

About that time, according to Don Ford, they heard
the women in the house screaming and Bobby went

back. "I was walking the rungs of a ladder to get up on the porch when the thing grabbed me."

. . . The "creature" was described by Ford as being about seven feet tall and about three feet wide across the chest. "At first I thought it was a bear but it runs upright and moves real fast. It is covered with hair," he said.

See what I mean? They're hell on shotguns in those Arkansas swamps. Heck, if you're short a scatter gun, the local authorities will bring you an extra!

What I didn't remember until I started writing this book is that a lot of Fouke locals appear in the 1973 film. Let me just say that explains a lot.

If you want to read what is considered to be the most thorough account of the whole history of the monster, take a look at *The Beast of Boggy Creek* by Lyle Blackburn (2012), available at that online bookstore named after a big river.

There are plenty of reasons to be skeptical about the Fouke Monster, but here's why the beast is important to me and my association with cryptozoology.

I had never even heard of Bigfoot when I saw that movie. When my Dad, in an effort to get me to quit sleeping with the light on — because everybody knows that seven-foot swamp monsters are scared of 60-watt bulbs — told me there were all kinds of legendary creatures around the world, a racehorse couldn't have beat me down to the library.

Yeah, remember, this was all pre-Internet, but I was hooked. Fast forward to 1981. Even though it's spelled a lot of different ways — thank you Ellis Island — my Cutty ancestors are all Scots and I had always wanted to see the old homeland.

Just after I got out of high school, and with a little help from my folks, I scraped together the money to go to Scotland.

And that's where it happened. On a perfectly clear, perfectly sober day in May, I saw my first and only cryptid — but I hope not my last, because I don't have any plans to be dead any time soon. Yeah, I know you're already ahead of me. I saw the Loch Ness Monster.

The Loch Ness Monster

If there's any unknown creature you can count on people knowing about, it's Nessie, although, there's no accounting for ignorance.

When the movie *Titanic* came out in 1997, I was sitting in a coffee shop eavesdropping on a genius and his significantly smarter girlfriend.

She was trying to get him to go see the flick and he was trying to get out of it, grumbling it was a chick thing.

She said, "Oh, come on, you'll like the part where the boat sinks." And he said, "You already know how it ends?"

I rest my case re: ignorance.

So, if you haven't heard about Nessie, here goes. Loch Ness is a lake in the Highlands of Scotland with no access to the sea — at least not since about 10,000 years ago.

Since 1933, when a famous photograph (now know to be a hoax) showed a creature looking very much like a dinosaur swimming in the lake, there have been regular sightings of "Nessie."

For the record, what I saw did not look like a dinosaur swimming. Okay, actually, before we go any farther, let me tell you what I did see.

My Own Nessie Sighting

It was 10 o'clock in the morning and I was riding toward the back of the tour bus sitting in a window seat. We were on our way to Drumnadrochit, a village on the north shore of Loch Ness at the head of Urquhart Bay.

I was just staring out the window wondering what we were going to get for lunch. The surface of the lake looked as smooth as glass.

Suddenly, a ripple disturbed the water. It caught my eye because as a kid I used to do a lot of fishing. Sometimes water snakes will come in and attack the fish on your stringer. What I was seeing out there on the calm lake looked exactly like one of those snakes heading toward me.

As I watched, two humps rose out of the water. I can't tell you how big they were because I had no frame of reference, but I could make out scales. The humps glided along for about 100 yards and then gradually receded under the water.

I turned to the guy I was sitting with, a fellow from Oklahoma, and from the look on his face, I already knew the answer to my question. "Did you see that?" I asked. He nodded dumbly and we quietly decided to keep the whole thing to ourselves rather than be the laughing stocks of the whole bus.

The next morning at breakfast, the guy joined me at my table and laid a newspaper down beside my plate. There had been Nessie sighting the day before all up and down the loch.

All these years later, I still believe that I saw a real creature in that loch and that someday its existence will be proven.

The Surgeon's Photo Forward

So, as I was saying, modern Nessie sightings started in 1933 when a London surgeon, Kenneth Wilson, claimed to have taken a photograph of the creature that was published in *The Inverness Courier*.

This one is so iconic, I have no doubt you'll recognize it instantly. Just go to images.google.com and type in "surgeon's photo Loch Ness."

You'll see a black-and-white, grainy image of a classic, long-necked "dinosaur" appearing to be swimming in the lake, looking out of the frame to the right. For many people this remains the definitive image of what Nessie looks like.

That picture, however, is now a proven hoax. It was nothing but a model "monster" built on a toy submarine. But for decades, the "Surgeon's Photo" was considered to be the best proof that a surviving species of dinosaur or giant water serpent lives in Loch Ness and it's one of the best known of all cryptid photographs.

Obviously if there is something living in the lake, it has to be more than one creature, which is completely possible. Loch Ness extends for some 23 miles / 37 kilometers and its deepest point is 745 feet / 227 meters.

That's a pretty decent volume of water and through the years people have theorized that the creatures must live in underwater caves, perhaps near the 13th-16th century ruins of Urquhart Castle adjacent to Drumnadrochit.

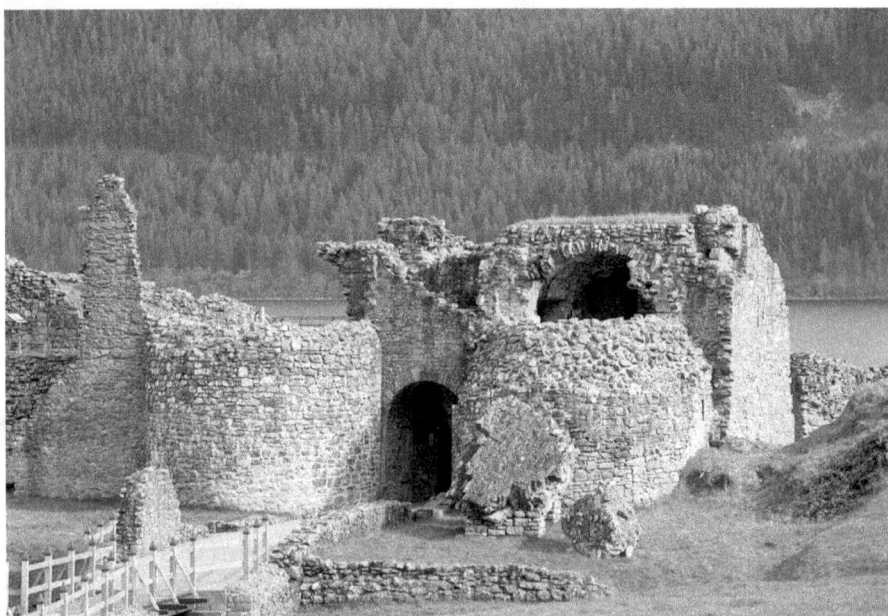

What I saw did not look like some dinosaur, so my money is on a more serpent-like animal. The lake is only 52 feet / 16 meters above sea level and was once open to ocean. If the creatures were already living or spawning in the lake, they probably just became trapped when that access was cut off and have continued doing their thing for centuries.

Skeptics contend that if that were true somebody would have caught an example of Nessie by now or there would have been a carcass washed up on the shore. That's never happened, yet the sightings persist.

There was a real surprise in 2013 when a satellite using the Apple mapping system got a picture of something about 100 feet / 30.48 meters long swimming in Loch Ness. The image shows something that looked a lot like a catfish to me, with two flippers clearly visible. It's easy to find, just go to images.google.com and search for "apple loch ness photo."

Needless to say The Official Loch Ness Monster Fan Club (www.LochNessSightings.com) was beyond thrilled with this "proof" — until digital enhancements of the image showed the "flippers" to be the wake of the boat that made up "Nessie's" body. The point of bringing up the image at all is how much people *want* there to be something in that lake.

In November 2014 a man named Richard Collis who has been fishing in Loch Ness for years took a two-minute video with his iPhone that appears to show a neck and head sticking up out of the water.

His own wife laughed when she saw the footage and said it couldn't possibly be a hoax, explaining that her husband isn't very "technical" and would never have been able to alter the image. Whatever is shown in the footage is about 500 feet / 152.4 meters offshore, so there's still nothing conclusive, but the story hit the news all the same.

I get that, because the Fouke Monster and Nessie hit my imagination in a big way. That day on a tour bus in Scotland, I became a true believer — not in any one "monster" in particular, but in the idea that not everything in our world has been discovered or is known.

People, seriously, you have to leave a little room for wonder in this life. Think I'm full of it about that? This is as good a place as any to point out that not all cryptids are actually a load of bull.

"Cryptids" That Really Do Exist

Some critters we think of as being pretty normal today were dismissed as so much hogwash when they were first sighted. The kangaroo, platypus, giant panda, and Komodo dragon all fall into that category.

- In 2001, the Sri Lankan Devil Bird or Ulama, long a staple of local folklore for its blood-curdling screams, was identified as the Spot-Bellied Eagle Owl (*Bubo nipalensis.*)

  The elusive, nocturnal creature was believed to be an omen of death with a voice like that of a woman wailing in inconsolable grief.

- In 1994 a scientist in Australia identified a new species of forest-dwelling marsupial called the Dingiso (*Dendrolagus mbaiso.*)

  The Dingiso is the creature behind the mythic Bondegezou or "man of the forests" once identified as a small, tree-climbing man covered in black-and-white fur and regarded by the Moni of Western Indonesia as an ancestral spirit.

My point? Just because the description of an unknown animal sounds strange and there's no physical proof *yet* doesn't mean the thing isn't out there. All that means is that we haven't *found* one. Personally, I'd prefer to live in a world where I think there are still some surprises and interesting stuff left to discover.

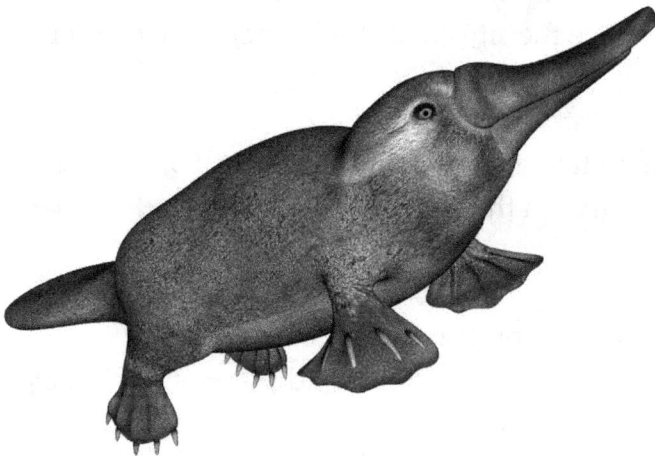

The cryptids in the rest of this book are either some of my personal favorites or I chose to include them because the stories associated with them make some point about cryptozoological inquiry I think is important.

That doesn't mean I'm going to go out in the woods or the swamp looking for them, but it does mean I won't be surprised if they turn up to be real one of these days.

You Don't Have to Hunt Monsters to Enjoy This Stuff

One thing that's kind of cool about the Internet is that it can take you a lot of places right from the comfort of your home. Throw Google Earth on your iPad and tell me how much time passes before you come up for air.

You don't have to out in the field in the middle of the night trying to call up Chupacabras to be actively interested in cryptozoology.

At the end of this book, I'll give you a long list of some of my favorite websites that will help you stay current in the field. I will add that the list is far from comprehensive, and I can't guarantee the sites will still be there when you look.

Things on the Internet come and go, and it can take a lot of energy to maintain a cryptozoology site. All of the sites listed were active in the summer of 2015 when this book was written.

There are also a ton of discussion boards that can be a lot of fun, but let me give you a really solid piece of advice. Do not get on one of those forums and jump into the conversation immediately. Lurk for a couple of weeks and get the lay of the land.

People lose their damn minds arguing about this stuff. Wait until you witness your first full-blown flame war in a forum if you don't believe me.

Be respectful on forums, and try to refrain from telling someone who has seen something by dark of night that they were drunk or that they're an idiot – even if they are drunk and they're an idiot. Remember that scared people have imaginations cranked up to nuclear-threat level.

If there's one thing I can affirm about the vast bulk of cryptid sightings, the people who are telling the story believe what they're saying. In my experience, the truthful folks outweigh the hoaxers.

Keep your sense of cynical perspective, but play nice when you start getting involved in the online world of cryptozoology.

Chapter 2 - Lake Creatures

As cryptids go, lake monsters are pretty darn popular. Most all of them are supposed to be left-over dinosaurs. In more recent years, however, you see a lot of mutant-crawling-out-of-the-chemical slime theories or stories about wild animals dumped in contained environments where they grew crazy big.

You know, crocodile vs. helicopter as per *Lake Placid*? (If this is one bad movie you haven't seen, get thee to Netflix and rent.)

Why are humans so intrigued with lake monsters? Because they live in an element where we can only survive for brief periods of time provided we didn't flunk Swimming 101. The water is not our natural habitat and even under the best of conditions, it can be a little scary.

Ask anyone who has ever gone swimming in a lake. There's nothing like that thrill of terror when something unseen under the surface brushes up against your leg.

Lake monsters tap into that sense of *something* lurking in the depths. And if there's one thing the lakes where most of these creatures are believed to be hiding have in common, it's depth.

Ogopogo

If you don't want to go all the way to Scotland in search of a lake monster, head to British Columbia's Lake Okanagan, home of Ogopogo or, as the native Salish called him, N'ha-a-itk.

Since the 19th century there have been reports of a serpent-like creature living in Lake Okanagan. The animal is most commonly described as 40-50 feet / 12-15 meters in length, dark, and featureless. Sometimes it has multiple humps, at others it's mistaken for a log.

The name "Ogopogo" was taken from a popular 1920s song describing a mythical critter that was a composite of the features of several animals. Kind of a Twenties, version of the One-Eyed, One-Horned, Flying Purple People Eater.

A song about an animal made of spare parts is actually a

good source for a name for this beast. "Reliable" witnesses have said the aquatic cryptid living in Okanagan has the head of a horse / sheep / seal / alligator and a nifty set of horns.

Lake Okanagan is an even bigger chunk of watery real estate than Loch Ness in terms of length — 84 miles / 135 km — and it's roughly 3 miles / 5 km wide. The average depth is 249 feet / 76 meters with the deepest hole extending to 761 feet / 232 meters.

Overall, however, Loch Ness is deeper. The average depth of the Loch is 433 feet / 132 meters. Still, Okanagan has plenty of places for a creature to live unseen and there is another crucial difference. You can't see squat in the water at Loch Ness because of all the peat in the soil.

Lake Okanagan is clear enough, however, that investigators have used a lot of high-tech underwater gizmos including remotely operated vehicles (ROVs) and even a mini sub to look for Ogopogo.

Understanding Lake Okanagan

The deepest parts of the lake have been explored by such underwater vehicles and nothing was found, but the sightings still persist. Why? Well, for one thing there's a lot of lumber floating around in Okanagan — as in thousands of logs harvested in the area's local timber industry.

The lake is known for its unusually long wave patterns. Run the waves up against the logs and you get some pretty

funky looking abnormalities in the water. Out there on the
surface of the lake, without anything to measure
perspective, even a duck hauling feathery ass can look
"monstrous."

The most famous Ogopogo film was shot in 1968 and
showed something churning up the lake water. When
National Geographic took a closer look at the footage in 2005,
the conclusion was that the photographer, Arthur Folden,
did spot an actual animal, but it was probably a beaver or a
waterfowl.

So what are people seeing in Okanagan? The really
reasonable folks say there's just some damned big sturgeon
in the lake. The accepted record for a freshwater sturgeon
catch was in an estuary of the Volga River in Russia.

The massive fish was 24 feet / 7.2 meters long and weighed 3,460 lbs. / 1571 kg. That catch was made in 1827, but expert anglers estimated that a really old sturgeon living in undisturbed water today might top 6,000 lbs. / 2721 kg.

Next time you're bored on a Saturday, binge watch a few episodes of *River Monsters.* Then try to convince me you'd go swimming anywhere near where those critters live!

Common Factoid: Any time the suggestion of a cryptid is brought up, a wildlife expert will step up and say, "No, no. What they're really seeing is X."

Later in the book we'll talk about the Jersey Devil, which game biologists say could be a great horned owl. Not that I've ever seen any seven-foot-tall owls, but you get the idea.

In some cases though, the plausible explanations are pretty good when you stop to look at them, and in this case, I think the sturgeon theory has some merit.

Still, it's cool to think Ogopogo could be some "extinct" prehistoric whale like a Basilosaurus as some people want us to believe.

The Basilosaurus, a marine mammal, lived 40-34 million years ago. The fossil record shows it was an animal that reached as much as 65 feet / 20 meters in length and had an elongated body that might have looked serpentine when the creature was swimming.

If you want to see some Ogopogo pictures and read about

the ongoing search to explain what, if anything, lives in Lake Okanagan, visit The Legend Hunters at www.ogopogoquest.com.

Champ

Now, let's move to an even bigger body of fresh water in terms of surface space. Lake Champlain runs 125 miles / 201 km in length with a maximum width of 14 miles / 23 km. It extends from Quebec in Canada through portions of New York and Vermont in the United States.

The average depth of the lake is only 64 feet / 19.5 meters. At its deepest point, the water drops down 400 feet / 122 meters, which means Lake Champlain is significantly shallower than either Loch Ness or Okanagan.

That does not, however, stop this massive body of water from claiming its own resident beastie! (To be honest, I think almost all large lakes have their own resident "monsters.")

Like Loch Ness, Lake Champlain was once connected to the Atlantic Ocean. Granted, that was about 10,000 years ago, but any former link to open water is very, very good in a cryptozoological sense.

The creature that purportedly lives in the lake, affectionately called "Champ," is one of the best-known lake monsters in North America after Ogopogo. In 1873, P.T. Barnum offered a $50,000 reward for Champ, dead or alive. (Of course, this is also the same guy who assured us that there's a sucker born every day.)

At any rate, the best evidence that something unusual swims in the Champlain waters is a photo taken in 1977.
The Mansi Photo

On July 5, 1977 Sandra Mansi, her husband Anthony, and their two children were driving along Lake Champlain. About noon, they stopped and walked out onto a small bluff overlooking the water. The kids went down to play in the water and Anthony went back to the car for their camera.

As Sandra was watching the children, she saw something moving in the water about 150 feet / 45.7 meters off shore. Without warning, a head and neck rose out of the water just as Anthony came up behind Sandra. He screamed for the kids to get out of the lake.

Sandra took the camera and snapped one photo. As she watched, the creature turned its head slightly and then slowly disappeared under the surface.

She guessed that the animal's neck had been sticking out of the water about 6 feet / 1.8 meters and that the visible part of the body was probably 12-15 feet / 3.7-4.6 meters long.

The whole encounter lasted around five minutes. Great evidence, right? Yeah. Well. There's no negative because Mansi says she always threw them away.

There aren't any more photos from the same roll. Mansi

can't find the place where it happened. And the family didn't release the picture for four years.

Like most of these kinds of images, the Mansi photograph has been analyzed six ways from Sunday. Some "experts" say it couldn't have been faked.

Others performing voodoo math say yes, the head and hump were big . . . or 50% smaller than Mansi suggested . . . or not connected . . . or a sand bar. You getting the idea here?

Common Factoid: Any time the photographer can't produce the negatives or the original, fresh-out-of-the-camera files of the image, be very suspicious.

Without the originals, there's no way to conclusively determine if the picture has been doctored. Now, I will say this. Back in the days of film, it wasn't all that unusual for people to throw negatives away.

My Mom pitched them all the time, so I'm not saying Mansi lied, I'm just saying her story would carry more weight if she had the negatives.

More Recent Evidence

Even with the dodgy aspects of the Mansi photo, the fact remains that stories about a creature living in the lake date back to local Abenaki and Iroquois legends. That could easily get written off to tribal mythology, but by 1992, the total number of modern sightings was tallied at 180 with some 600 individual eyewitnesses involved.

In July 2014, cryptozoologists Dennis Hall and Katy Elizabeth, working with a hydrophone system in a portion of the lake called Scotch Bonnet, recorded a series of clicking noises they believe is evidence that something in the water is using echolocation.

What the heck is echolocation?

It's a way to use sound to get around. Even some blind people can learn to use it. Basically you listen to the sound wave as it bounces back at you and use the echo to navigate around (or find) objects in low-visibility conditions.

The Likely Suspects

Hall and Elizabeth's theory about Champ is that a surviving dinosaur, the Tanystropheus, which lived 233 million years ago, is calling Lake Champlain home.

The reptile, which dates to the Middle Triassic period, had an extremely elongated neck that was at least 10 feet / 3 meters long. The animal's overall body length was 20 feet / 6 meters.

Other investigators go with the Basilosaurus theory that is also applied to Ogopogo because fossil evidence of the creature has been found just miles from Lake Champlain near Charlotte, Vermont.

The Basilosaurus (or Zeuglodon) was a species of whale

that lived in the late Eocene period 40-34 million years ago. It measured 40-65 feet / 12-20 meters in length and had a longer body that put it more in line with the "floating log" descriptions of Ogopogo.

The major contender to explain Nessie is some type of Plesiosaur, a group of long-necked marine reptiles dating to the Triassic period some 205 million years ago.

There were several types of Plesiosaur, and the animals were even more common during the Jurassic period. They are believed to have gone extinct 66 million years ago.

Since Plesiosaurs were distributed across all the world's oceans, they're always a good bet for any body of water that was once connected to the sea.

Common Factoid: I'm convinced that people have a *Jurassic Park* complex. Even though that whole island theme park "thing" in the movie didn't turn out well, folks still *want* some dinosaurs to be alive and hiding *somewhere*.

Never mind that if they were, they'd probably be eating us like chicken wings. Lots and lots of crypids are explained as living dinosaurs, or in the case of the two-legged types, the "missing link."

The major problem with theorizing that any of these pre-historic animals live in any of these lakes is the matter of breeding population.

Some theorists say you'd have to have at least 50 animals to get a healthy genetic distribution that would allow for long-term survival. If there were 50 of any of these critters in any of these lakes, people should be seeing them all the time.

Does that mean I think all these lake monsters are bogus? No. I saw one and other people are seeing something and until somebody conclusively proves that Nessie, Ogopogo, and Champ *aren't* real, anything is possible.

I've only hit the high points here. If you want to investigate other lake monsters, you can try:

- The Serpent in Seneca Lake in New York
- Old Greeny, also in New York in Cayuga Lake
- Som in Lake Somyn in the Ukraine
- Manipogo in Lake Manitoba or Winnipogo in Lake Winnipegosis
- Cressie in Newfoundland's Crescent Lake
- Igopogo in Ontario's Lake Simcoe
- Mussie in Ontario's Muskrat Lake
- The White River Monster in Arkansas also called Whitey
- Tahoe Tessie in Lake Tahoe
- Slimy Slim in Fulks Lake in Indiana
- Kipsy in the Hudson River in New York
- Bessie in Lake Erie
- The North Shore Monster in the Great Salt Lake in Utah
- The Lukwata in Lake Victoria in Kenya
- Eachy in Bassenthwaite Lake in England
- Morag in Loch Morar in Scotland
- Mukie in the Lake of Killarney in Ireland
- Issie in Lake Ikeda in Japan
- Bunyip in Lake Modewarre in Victoria, Australia

And that's not even a complete list!

Chapter 3 - Sea Creatures

It stands to reason if people are seeing things in lakes, they must also be spotting sea monsters. This isn't a category of cryptid I've looked at all that extensively, but there are some interesting cases I think are worth mentioning, as a contrast to the lake beasties if nothing else.

Caddy

Here's one from the Pacific Northwest, for instance, that was completely new to me. Since the 1930s, from Alaska down through Oregon, there have been reports of a "Cadborosaurus," a name that, from what I can tell, was made up by a newspaper editor.

The creature is popularly called "Caddy" and seems to be most active around Vancouver Island and particularly in Cadboro Bay, near Victoria, British Columbia.

The physical details fall in line with the lake "monsters" we've already talked about:

- 15-45 feet / 5-14 meters in length
- serpent-like body often seen as "humps"
- long neck with a horse-like head
- side flippers
- fast swimming

Frankly, if this is some left-over dinosaur, the waters off the Pacific Northwest make more sense as a home range than an inland lake. The coastline up there is rugged with lots of hidden bays and inlets. The Cascadia ocean basin lying offshore has a maximum depth of 9,600 feet / 2,930 meters.

Other supposed sea "serpents" around the world include the:

- Con Rit in Vietnam and Algeria, a sort of aquatic centipede
- Kaijin in Japan, a sea dwelling hominid
- Akkorokamui, also in Japan, specifically Funka Bay in Hokkaido, a giant octopus-like thingie
- Megalodon, a giant shark swimming the world's oceans
- Steller's Sea Ape, a creature with the head of a hog and the tail of a shark

And ya gotta love the Caballo Marino Chilote out of Chile. It's an *invisible* cryptid only folks with magical powers can see. If you have the mojo, you're looking at a long-snouted, golden-maned horse with four fins and a fish tail.

Apparently there are dwarf and giant variaties, but I'm unclear if that changes how *much* magical power you need to log a sighting.

The Ocean: Ultimate Hiding Place

Many of these stories about sea monsters grow up after a carcass washes ashore that cannot be identified. The problem with this kind of "evidence" is the effect of saltwater and scavengers on the remains.

Typically scientists can look at such floating road kill and come up with a reasonable explanation to ID the carcass, but there's no denying a lot of the stuff pulled out of the water will, on first glance, scare the bejeebers out of a person.

Even the biggest skeptic should be onboard with the notion that we really don't have a clue about what's living down there at the bottom of the ocean — or "still living" as the case may be. You know that whole "final frontier" *Star Trek* line?

The ocean is truly the earth's last frontier and the farther man can travel into its depths, the stranger things we're going to find.

Considering that 71% of the surface of the earth is covered by the oceans, which contain 80% of all life on the planet, we don't know squat about the real aquatic census. What we do know is that there are more fish species than mammals, reptiles, and birds combined.

Of those? Scientists figure that in the really deep regions of the ocean there are about 10 million species that haven't been seen or named yet.

How's that for cryptids?

Life Forms in the Deep Ocean

Uh, yeah. It's estimated that 98% of all species in the ocean live on the bottom – and sometimes the bottom can be pretty danged *bottomless*.

An ROV snapped a picture of a Bigfin Squid off the coast of Oahu in 2001 at a depth of 2.1 miles / 3.38 km! The creature, trailing tentacles and all, was 13-16 feet / 4-5 meters in length.

The Challenger Deep at the south end of the Mariana Trench in the Pacific Ocean goes down 36,200 feet / 6.85 miles / 11.02 km as compared to the average global ocean depth of 12,144 feet / 2.3 miles / 3.7 km.

At that depth, according to *National Geographic*, the pressure is akin to being under a pile of 50 jumbo jets (8 tons per square inch.)

On December 6, 2014, at a depth of 5 miles / 8 km in the Mariana Trench, images were captured of a 6-inch / 15 cm snailfish with big wing-like fins and a long, undulating tail.

Researchers lured the fish into camera view with bait, but they didn't have any way to catch it, so they couldn't decide if it's a new species or not. Regardless, this critter is the current record holder for being alive at the deepest level of the ocean.

Right now scientists think it's impossible for fish to live below a depth of 26,900 feet / 5.09 miles / 8.19 km because their cells can't produce enough of a substance called osmolyte to help them take the crushing pressure.

Alan Jamieson, a deep-sea biologist at Aberdeen University, who was one of the leaders of the expedition that snagged the photo told *National Geographic*, "If a fish can go deeper, it's different from any other fish on the planet." Which is as far as Mother Nature is concerned, the equivalent of saying, "Bring it!"

New England Sea Monsters

Okay, so now that we've established the ocean's great potential as a hiding place for cryptids, you're not going to be surprised that a lot of the stories come from places where a seafaring way of life is pretty much the norm, like New England.

In the 18th century, the whaling industry was front and center in the life of the region. Predictably, there were all kinds of sightings of sea monsters up and down the Atlantic coast. Most originated in Maine or Massachusetts. Sea "serpents" have been spotted in Broad, Penobscot, Portland, and Casco Bays in Maine.

One of the more flamboyant of these stories occurred in 1779 when Commander Edward Preble rowed out into Penobscot Bay to confront one such creature, firing bullets at the ten feet / 3.05 meters of the animal's body that rose out of the water.

The animal wisely swam quickly in the other direction, but this creature, often called "Cassie" after Casco Bay, was still being seen well into the 1950s. There have been fewer sightings in the last half-century, perhaps attributable to the amount of traffic in those waters now.

(Around Chesapeake Bay, a similar creature is called "Chessie," with another thought to be living near Gloucester.)

Common Factoid: Pretty much everyone who encounters a cryptid is a lousy shot. Man, I cannot tell you how many of these stories contain some variation on the line, "I shot at the creature and missed." This either means (a) the eyewitness wants to sound badass because in reality they turned and ran or (b) all cryptids are bullet proof.

Giant Squid

Stories of gigantic squid have been around since Ancient Greece. Remember that back then the mapmakers just wrote in "here be dragons" for the unknown regions of the earth. Explorers setting out in rinky-dink little boats had good reason to fear bigger things out there in the open water.

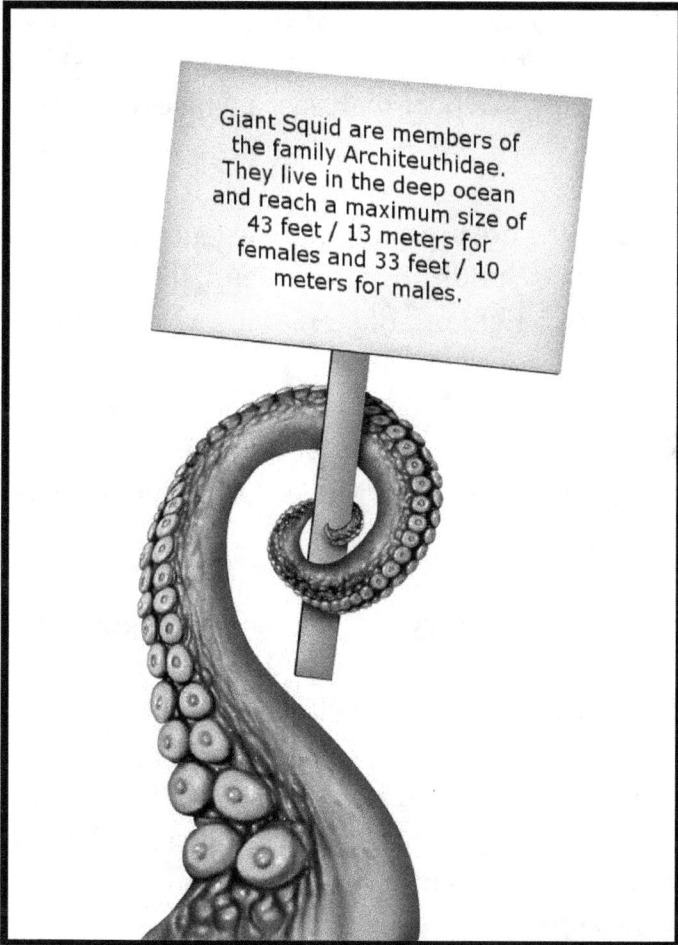

Giant Squid are members of the family Architeuthidae. They live in the deep ocean and reach a maximum size of 43 feet / 13 meters for females and 33 feet / 10 meters for males.

Remember the *Nina, Pinta,* and *Santa Maria* from your schoolbooks? Yeah, Columbus and his men took off to discover the "new" world on ships that were about 50 feet / 15.24 meters long.

A Blue Whale measures 98 feet / 30 meters and tips the scales at 200 short tons / 180 tonnes. Kind of getting why Moby Dick had the advantage over Ahab?

(For the record, *Moby Dick* was supposed to be a Sperm Whale. They average 50-60 feet / 17-20 meters and weigh 40-50 tons / 36-45 tonnes. Nantucket whalers like the *Pequod* were about 87 feet / 26.5 meters. So, yeah, I was just being a wise ass, but still, in a boat that size, a whale qualifies as a monster.)

The Kraken is the great-granddaddy legend of this Giant Squid bunch of cryptids. Big as an island, the tentacles of the Kraken reach right out of Norse legend and into the present day.

If you saw *Clash of the Titans* in 1981, you know the Kraken as the servant of the gods on Mount Olympus. (It also showed up in *Pirates of the Caribbean* in 2006.)

In the hands of the Hollywood special effects guys, the Kraken in *Titans* became a beast with a human top half and crab-like legs, but there were still plenty of tentacles.

But, regardless of where or how the Kraken is portrayed, this beast is the genesis of the giant squid cryptid and was actually the inspiration for both *Moby Dick* and *20,000 Leagues Under the Sea*.

This, however, is one of those cases where a real creature actually can claim the title of Giant Squid. In 2004, a team of Japanese researchers managed to photograph a living example.

Although the creatures are highly elusive, it's now known that they do reach lengths of 30-40 feet / 9.14-12.19 meters. Now *that* is some serious calamari!

Megalodon

People are just freaking fascinated by sharks. I know folks who basically stop *everything* for Shark Week on the Discovery Channel. And there is absolutely no other explanation for a flick like *Sharknado* but shark obsession.

As far as I can tell with this crowd the bigger the shark the better. There a lot of big sharks on record that are not cryptids, but they are monsters.

In the 1970s a Great White was caught off Phillip Island in Australia that was 21 feet / 6.2 meters long and weighed 5,085 lbs. / 2306 kg.

I'm with Chief Brodie. I see one of those damn things in the water (a) I want back and dry land and (b) if that isn't an option, I damn well do want a bigger boat.

So, given this insanity, is there any wonder why some people love the idea that there are Megalodons swimming around out there?

The Megalondon is a real creature, by the way. They exist in the fossil record, but they're supposed to have all been extinct since the Cenozoic Era about 15.9 to 2.6 million years ago. They make *Jaws* look like a minnow with anemia.

The current consensus among scientists is that the Megalodon measured 79-82 feet / 24-25 meters in length. Some of the teeth that have been recovered were 7.25 inches / 184.1 millimeters in height. Their calculated bite force would be about ten times that of a Great White Shark.

So, what are the chances these things are still living in deep ocean waters? Well, in 1875 two Megalodon teeth were recovered that were dated to just 10,000 to 14,000 years ago. By that time, the big sharks should have been extinct, but very likely weren't.

In 1918, a group of fishermen in Australia reported an encounter with a shark they insisted was 115 feet / 35.05 meters in length. The witnesses were all experienced seamen who should have been able to tell the difference between a whale and a shark.

Pop over to YouTube and do a search for "megalodon sighted in Mariana Trench."

The 1:06 minute black-and-white clip complete with nifty Japanese subtitles and narration shows something pretty danged massive coming in the right side of the frame. Then, look at "Megalodon Found! Do Megalodon The Monster Shark Live." This second video is 15 minutes in length and has some intriguing moments.

In the first few frames, which is some footage shot in Brazilian waters, you'll see something swim by in the upper right-hand corner that does not look like a whale. That segment is followed by Australian news footage showing a 12.14 foot / 3.7 meter shark with big bites taken out of its torso.

The estimated size on the shark that bit down on the 12-footer is 16.4 feet / 5 meters, which goes to prove that no matter how big you are, there's always someone higher up on the food chain.

There's a lot of overblown music in the video, but also some interesting size comparison images of what a Megalodon would look like – think Greyhound bus. If nothing else, treat yourself to the trash talk in the comments.

Most Megalodon sightings are written off as mistaken identification of basking sharks or whales, but there's evidence to suggest that there are bigger sharks living today than anyone who has seen *Jaws* would like to consider.

As we've clearly established, the oceans are vast. In 2012, man's deepest descent was achieved by the Deepsea Challenger, reaching down 35,814 feet / 10,916 meters. That's 6.7 miles / 10.78 km.

The pilot of the craft was film director James Cameron, who produced a documentary about his experience that came out in August 2014. (Apparently making *Titanic* turned him into a deep water junkie. The wreck of the ocean liner sits at a measly 12,500 feet / 2.36 miles / 3.8 km.)

If you want to learn more about the dive, go to www.DeepSeaChallenge.com. It's pretty danged impressive.

Once you've seen it, I think you'll agree almost anything could be living down there. Is the Megalodon one of those things? Possibly, but there is one simple argument that gives us a resounding negative answer.

If the Megalodon were alive today, he'd be at the absolute top of the aquatic food chain and would be snacking on whales like crazy. If the massive sharks had survived into modern times, people should be seeing them in the vicinity of whale pods.

Also, whale carcasses should be washing up routinely, which they do, often with large chunks taken out of them. Most of those animals are killed by ships or by other whales and the damage that's seen by the time the carcass reaches the beach is from scavengers.
But here's the last nail in the Magalodon coffin as far as I'm

concerned. They're supposed to be hiding in the deep oceans, right? Most of the really deep water in the ocean hovers at a temperature of 32-36.5 degrees F / 0-3 degrees C.

The Megalodon was a warm water animal. Unless he's taken to wearing a heated wet suit, I don't think he's hanging out in water that cold.

Are unknown monsters in the depths? Absolutely. Scientists do not dispute that. Is the Megalodon one of them? No.

Chapter 4 - Bigfoot and Other Hominids

The cryptid hominids capture our imagination because of that whole "missing link" thing. (Go to one of my family reunions and you can get the answer to that one.)

Of course Bigfoot and the Yeti top the list in this category, but there are also some other "man like" creatures out there that I'll discuss at the end of the chapter.

Bigfoot

If you've never heard of any other cryptid, Bigfoot, like Nessie, probably exists in your frame of reference. Up in Canada, they call him Sasquatch, and down in Florida, he's the Skunk Ape.

I'm not going to get into the debate about whether or not those names refer to a completely different species of cryptid. I just want to simplify things and say that there are reports all over North America of a large unidentified hominid with a high concentration of encounters originating in the Pacific Northwest.

The First Famous Bigfoot Tracks

On October 5, 1958 the *Humboldt Times* in California ran a photo of Jerry Crew, a construction worker, holding the plaster cast of a footprint he found in Bluff Creek Valley. That story was the first use of the name Bigfoot.

If you want to head straight into the epicenter of Bigfoot

country make for Oregon, Washington, and British Columbia, although the creatures are said to range into northern California and Idaho as well.

That's rugged territory covered by vast, largely untouched forests. Just like the deep oceans would provide excellent cover for a surviving dinosaur, the Pacific Northwest could well shelter an undocumented hominid.

Heck, if things get much worse in the world, I'm heading up there to go off-grid and the cryptozoologists will be spotting me!

The Basic Bigfoot Description

The classic Bigfoot description is of a creature that stands erect on two legs reaching a height of 6-9 feet / 1.83-2.74 meters. Although the body is stocky with a barrel-like torso, the head is pointed and small with no discernible forehead.

The face is light in color and possibly hairless, darkening with age. The small eyes sit beneath a prominent brow ridge. The entire body, including the cranium, is covered in shaggy dark hair that is red-brown, but may silver with age.

The tracks after which the creature is named are generally 14-16 inches / 35.56-40.64 cm in length, with five toes and a width of 7 inches / 17.78 cm.

Kidnapped by Bigfoot

There are two major "milestone" events in the history of the Bigfoot legend and about a jillion inconsequential sightings by folks clearly under the influence of adult beverages. So let's start with Albert Ostman of British Columbia.

In 1924, Ostman said he was captured by a family of four giant creatures that resembled apes while camping at Toba Inlet across from Vancouver Island. The creatures held him in a canyon for six days. They were friendly, and made no attempt to harm Ostman, who came forward with his story in 1957.

Experts who interviewed the man, including John Napier, an anthropologist from the Smithsonian, found him both sane and sincere. When this story was included in a couple of magazine articles in the Fifties, Roger Patterson was inspired to go out looking for the creatures and shot a piece of film that is still hotly debated today.

The Patterson Film

The Patterson Film, recorded on October 20, 1967 near Bluff Creek, California shows an apelike creature approximately 7 feet / 2.13 meters in height walking away from the camera.

Before the animal, lovingly dubbed Patty (it's supposed to be a female Bigfoot) disappears into the trees, she stops and looks back at the camera.

Patterson and his companion, Bob Gimlin, tracked the creature for three miles before they lost the trail. Nine days later, casts were made of a series of ten footprints found at the site that measured 14.5 inches / 36.83 cm in length with a width of 6 inches / 17.78 cm.

Over the past 30 years, the film has been examined multiple times. Although widely charged with being a hoax perpetrated with an ape suit made by John Chambers, the make-up artist who later won an Academy Award for his work on *Planet of the Apes* in 1968, the Patterson footage remains controversial.

Until his death, Chambers denied any involvement in a hoax, and there are convincing arguments that the movement of the creature in the film displays complex muscular action that would not have been possible through any type of suit.

You'll have zero problems locating this one. Just go to YouTube and type in "Patterson bigfoot footage." Watch to your heart's content – the original, the stabilized version, and the multiple analyzed versions. Have a freaking marathon.

I've watched a goodly number of these and I honestly can't make up my mind. Just about the time I'm ready to call it a guy in an ape suit, some expert starts talking about stride patterns and I'm convinced again. Regardless, this is one of the most compelling pieces of cryptid footage ever.

In September 2014 a researcher named M.K. Davis was able to stabilize Frame 61 of the footage sufficiently to show the creature's toes. That doesn't completely rule out the "guy in a suit" theory, but it would have to be one heck of a sophisticated suit for 1967 – even better than the costumes in *Planet of the Apes*.

There's no shortage of Bigfoot reports, and YouTube is pretty much awash in evidence. If you want to keep up with what's being done in this arena, take a look at:

- BigfootHub.com

- Brfro.net (Bigfoot Field Researchers Organization)
- NABigfootSearch.com (North American Bigfoot Search)
- BigfootLunchClub.com

Now, mainly because I need a nice transition here, Roger Patterson wrote and self-published a book in 1966 entitled *Do Abominable Snowmen Really Exist?*, which moves us along to the next majorly famous cryptid hominid.

The Yeti

The fabled "Abominable Snowmen" has long been one of the major players in the field of cryptozoology. Reports of upright, hairy, ape-like creatures are found throughout the Himalayas.

The creature more properly called the Yeti or the Meh-Teh came to popular attention in 1921 thanks to a report by Lt. Col. C.K. Howard-Bury, the leader of the British Mount Everest reconnaissance mission.

Howard-Bury and his party used binoculars to watch several dark forms moving across a snowfield at an elevation of 20,000 feet / 6096 meters. They discovered unexplained tracks that their sherpa guides said were made by the "metoh-kangmi," which translates roughly to "wild man of the snows."

Now, there's always the notion that the sherpas could have been having fun screwing around with the uptight Brits, but there's a lot more to the Yeti legend than that single encounter.

Although the 1921 account was more widely publicized, explorer B.H. Hodgson described a tall, bipedal creature in northern Nepal in 1832, and Laurence Waddell reported the discovery of footprints in 1899.

Like his North American brother, the Bigfoot, the Yeti is reputedly a large humanoid creature covered in thick, dark fur (not white as the cartoons would have us believe). In fact, this guy is so shaggy the hair is supposed to hang down all the ways to his knees.

The Yeti Meets the Modern World

In the 20th century, more and more people attempted to climb Mount Everest. The feat was not actually accomplished until May 29, 1953 when Sir Edmund Hillary and his guide Tenzing Norgay reached the summit.

I can't help but point out that until that day, and on many occasions after, there have been a lot of oxygen-starved adrenaline junkies wandering around up there on the mountain. Hallucinations are not out of the equation here.

Even Hillary said he saw prints up there on the high slopes, but later discounted any truth to the Yeti legend. Tensing Norgay believed in the Yeti because his father claimed to have seen the creature twice. Tensing reported looking at big footprints, but had no eyewitness experience himself.

Most of the Yeti accounts I've read are pretty much the

same, inexplicable footprints. I was a little amused to see that Jimmy Stewart (yeah, that one, the actor) is supposed to have smuggled a Yeti hand out of India in 1959. The so-called Pangboche Hand is from a Buddhist monastery in Nepal.

The Pangboche Hand

Oilman and adventurer Tom Slick photographed the Pangboche Hand in 1957. In 1959, an associate of Slick's Peter Byrne, pinched some of the bones and got them over the border into India, where they came into Stewart's possession.

Apparently Stewart just happened to be on a trip to India with his wife. They were staying in Calcutta, and Peter Byrne was a family friend. He convinced Stewart to wrap the bones up in Gloria's lingerie and get them out of the country in his luggage.

The couple's luggage was held by British customs, but English good manners prevailed. Mrs. Stewart's case was not opened, and the smuggling caper was a success.

Pieces of the Pangboche Hand were tested in 1960 and it was suggested that the discovery was really the frozen appendage of a Neanderthal man.

In 1991, NBC's *Unsolved Mysteries* managed to get ahold of some tissue samples, which were found to be "near human."

But then the entire hand, or what was left of it, disappeared from the monastery, so the whole thing went up in the air again until 2011 when a finger turned up. This time testing revealed the presence of human DNA.

Now, the only thing more plentiful up in those mountains than living oxygen-deprived climbers is dead, frozen ones. I don't find it all that surprising that a hand with human DNA would turn up, but the trail of evidence is so dodgy on this one, we're in the territory of Catholic saint relics as far as I'm concerned.

An Unknown Bear Species?

The more compelling evidence suggests that hair samples and some of the better footprint casings suggest a surviving species of bear in the region. This is actually one theory I can get behind.

When a grizzly bear stands up, he's a good 8 feet / 2.5 meters tall. Some polar bears will go 10 feet / 3.05 meters! That's abominably monstrous in my book!

In 2013, hairs collected in Northern India were compared to samples in the international repository of gene sequences, the GenBank, and came back as a match for an ancient polar bear.

To me, that's cooler than some big ape running around up in the high mountains. Bryan Sykes, the professor who headed up the analysis effort, told the BBC in October 2013,

"I think this bear, which nobody has seen alive, may still be there and may have quite a lot of polar bear in it."

If the Yeti does pan out to be a bear, or even a bear-hybrid previously unknown or thought to be extinct, it will prove the very thing about cryptozoology I love. It's the study of the *possibility* of unidentified, but very real animals.

> ***Common Factoid:*** While DNA testing may have been very good for O.J., it's even better for cryptozoology. Scientists have the ability to figure out if what people are seeing are one-shot hybrids of local animals, or a thriving population of some entirely new species. Any time I see a case where samples are sent in for DNA sequencing, I get very interested.

Skunk Ape

The Skunk Ape is worth setting apart from the normal run of Bigfoot stories for two reasons. The accounts come almost exclusively from the Florida Everglades and a really recent event will give me a good place to talk about fakers.

First things first. The major difference between this beast and Bigfoot is that the Skunk Ape is supposed to absolutely reek. The theory is that the odor, which is akin to rotten eggs or methane, is a by-product of the animal's habit of hiding out in alligator dens full of rotting kills.

Size wise, the Skunk Ape is in line with the Bigfoot legend, standing 6-7 feet / 1.83-2.13 meters with an estimated weight of 450 lbs. / 204.1 kg.

Reports have been fairly frequent, with a real rash in the 1960s and 1970s when the Skunk Ape was apparently roaming into the Dade County suburbs.

At the time, detractors said eyewitnesses were really seeing black bears -- a standard explanation for a lot of Skunk Ape sightings -- but one or two more recent encounters are a little more puzzling.

Skunk Ape Photos

In 2000 a woman who chose to remain anonymous mailed a couple of photos to the Sarasota County sheriff's office. She said they were taken in her backyard.

On three separate nights what the woman took to be an escaped orangutan came into her backyard to take apples she left for it off her back porch. Researchers were able to track the images to a photo lab located in a drugstore and thus determined they were likely taken at a home near the Myakka River.

Since then there have been several encounters in the area around the Myakka River State Park. In March 2013, Mike Falconer and his son pulled over to watch something wandering around in a field at the park and shot a short cellphone video of what they believed to be a Skunk Ape.

Several other cars pulled over as well, so they weren't the only ones to notice something out there in the field.

It's hard to make out anything definitive in the video, which is available on YouTube. Just search for "Myakka Skunk Ape."

In the 3:07 minute footage, you can't see squat until the subtitles tell you that the Falconers decided to try to get closer. There's some standard jumpy slogging through the field scenes, again with nothing clearly visible.

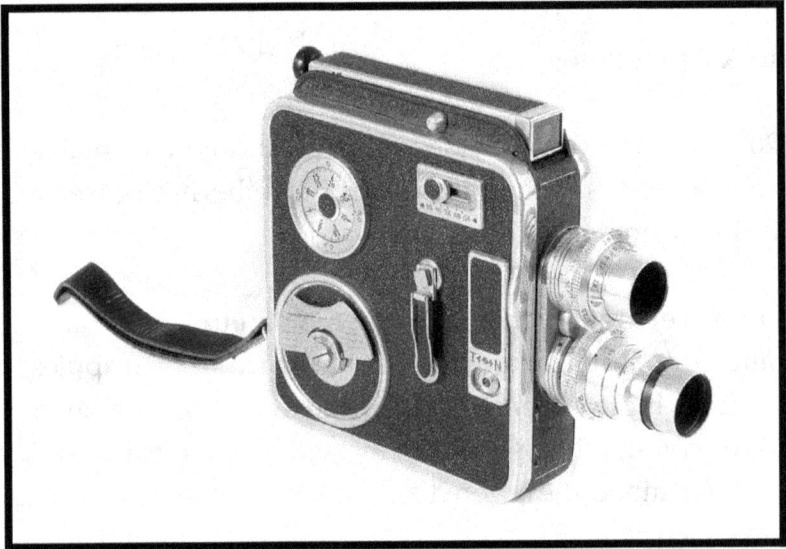

At that point, Falconer says he stopped filming and took stills with his iPhone 4s. Thankfully he's drawn a circle around the black speck in the distance that's supposed to be the Skunk Ape.

Probably the best still is at 2:42 on the YouTube video. About the best I'm willing to say is that something was out there and it was attracting the attention of passersby. The point in favor of the validity of this encounter is that

Falconer wasn't out there looking for anything. He was just a guy driving along who saw something strange. (And a lot of other people pulled over because they saw the same thing.)

Things get more interesting, however, when you realize there was another sighting in the park a few months later in September 2014. Same scenario. A motorist, this time a woman, just driving along minding her own business.

A researcher with the Bigfoot Field Researchers Organization (BFRO) interviewed her. She described a bipedal creature than ran about 15 feet / 4.57 meter in front of her car.

She saw a human-like face with a flat nose and tan leathery skin. The body was covered in black, shaggy fur. Amazingly, she got out of the car to have a look around and said she smelled the telltale odor.

The Lettuce Lake Hoax

As recently as February 2015 a Skunk Ape sighting made the news when Matthew McKamey, 28, spotted one of the creatures while canoeing at Lettuce Lake Park in January. He said he thought he had taken video of a bear until a park ranger told him the animals don't really wander into the swamps.

Yes, you guessed it, the footage is on YouTube. Search for "The Lettuce Lake Skunk Ape." The video is put up by Parabreakdown and has some nifty narration discussing the potential authenticity of the video.

You get both the original and a stabilized, enhanced version. The conclusion is that the images are "compelling."

I'll agree with that, and I'll agree with the observation of the narrator that if somebody wanted to perpetrate a hoax bad enough to get in water full of gators and water moccasins, more power to them!

But you know what? There are morons walking among us who would do just that, and in this case, apparently did.

While McKamey and his cohorts may have done a nice job of making a credible looking video, they left a lot of tracks behind them, including their interest in a scheduled Bigfoot conference.

You can read the whole account on the The Florida BFRO site (bfrofl.com) in an article entitled, "The Debunking of the Lettuce Lake Skunk Ape Footage."

Among other details in the lengthy and well-documented piece, the author, R. Monteith, reveals that McKamey is a musician and he's in a band with a guy who makes Bigfoot masks and "things."

Cryptozoology in the Age of Technology

Uh yeah. Okay then. So why bring this one up, Rex, if it's a big fat fake?

Because it's possible in this day and age to create video and images far more sophisticated than some of the most famous cryptid hoaxes like the Surgeon's Photo of the Loch Ness monster.

Yes, everyone has a smartphone with a camera and they're snapping photos of all kinds of stuff, but that does not make the evidence *real*.

Those same smartphones could easily be packed with .99 cent photo editing apps that can pull off some incredible and realistic effects.

We are now technologically in a better position to locate and prove the existence of cryptids than we've ever been before. Unfortunately, the fakers are also armed with the same nifty toys.

I, for one, like the skeptics. I want "proof" subjected to rigorous testing. If I'd just seen the Lettuce Lake video and not gone on to search for "Lettuce Lake hoax," I would have missed the article on the Florida BFRO site.

The bottom line is this. Be interested in cryptozoology, but don't be a gullible sap. This is one hobby that should come along with a healthy dose of "I don't believe a damn thing until you show me one alive or dead."

Now, all that being said, the Everglades, like all the other potential cryptid environments we've discussed are dense, harsh, and isolated. This kind of territory is the perfect hiding place for a reclusive creature to live undiscovered and unmolested. We're talking territory that covers 734 square miles / 1900 square kilometers.

I'm not saying the Skunk Ape couldn't be real. I am saying that McKamey didn't see one and like a bonehead, he pulled a stunt that will make it even harder for the next guy who sees something to get anyone to believe him.

The Orang Pendek

Since we just talked hoaxes, I thought we'd end this chapter with a cryptid primate I thing stands a real good chance of being proven to exist. Unlike Bigfoot, the Yeti, and the Swamp Ape, the Orang Pendek is a small animal possibly related to the orangutan.

The Orang Pendek has been spotted for years in Sumatra. A Dutch explorer had an encounter in October 1923 on the island of Poleloe Rimau. Although the man said he had a clear field of fire at the beast, he couldn't bring himself to take the shot because the creature looked so much like a human being.

Most people who say they've run into the Orang Pendek seem to feel the same way. In 1997 a trail cam supposedly snagged a shot of an ape-like animal with a long mane of red hair walking almost completely upright.

Described in newspaper accounts as "man's nearest cousin," the picture re-ignited theories that the Orang Pendek is indeed the long-fabled missing link.

Unfortunately, the stories were incorrect. There was no photograph. The bulk of the evidence on this cryptid comes from locals who say they see an animal that stands about 4 feet / 1.22 meters tall.

Biologists and botanists working in the area continue to gather information, and my money is on this critter eventually making it into the "proven to be real" column.

Why? Because it's easier for a 4 foot / 1.22 meter primate to hide in the jungles of Sumatra than it is for a 6-7 foot / 1.83-2.13 meter "monster" to live in near vicinity to man and not be seen.

Chapter 5 – Cryptid Canines

When you start talking cryptid canines, the first thing that comes to anybody's mind is your classic werewolf. In fact, the Michigan Dogman I'll discuss in this chapter is sometimes described as a werewolf.

That's not a definition I want to embrace, however, because if you really want to be a lycanthrope purist, a werewolf is a man cursed to turn into a wolf on the full moon. Think Lon Chaney in *The Wolfman* in 1941 or the hideous 2010 remake with Benicio del Toro

The strange canines people claim to see don't change forms. They may howl at a full moon, but they're not changed by it. (Any more than any of the rest of us that is. Ask an ER

nurse how nuts it gets on a full moon)
Technically, no one is really sure if El Chupacabra is a
canine, but since the most recent forensic testing in Texas of
strange, hairless creatures with leathery blue-gray skin say
"dog," that's where we're putting El Chupa.

El Chupacabra

Okay, you had to know it would be in here. Let's talk
chupacabra. Does this mean anything to you?

> **Scully**: You're not going to tell me you think it's that
> Mexican goat sucker thing.

> **Mulder**: El Chupacabra? No, they got four fangs, not
> two, and they suck goats, hence the name.

Yep. First time I heard of the Chupacabra was in an *X-Files*
episode, "El Mundo Gira," that aired on January 12, 1997.
(For the purists, the dialog above is from the classic ep "Bad
Blood" that aired February 22, 1998.)

Puerto Rico Reports

As cryptids go, El Chupa as he's lovingly known, is pretty
young, with the first attacks reported in March 1995 in
Puerto Rico.

The initial report stray over into the livestock mutation
phenomenon (that's typically one for the UFO groupies).
Eight sheep (or goats, depending on the source) were found
dead due to exsanguination (all their blood was drained

away) from three small puncture wounds to the chest. There were so many reports in 1995 that the Puerto Rican government actually put civil defense officials in charge of the investigation. All the resulting photos show various types of farm animals that were completely drained of blood through puncture wounds.

The Puerto Rican version of the Chupacabra is an animal that stands on its hind legs and has the requisite glowing red eyes. It has a line of spikes down the back — or at least on the upper back along the shoulders — and is hairless.

Many people have said the thing looks like a gargoyle come to life, and at least one report places the Chupacabra perched on the balcony of a home looking inside. Sightings soon spread to Chile, Nicaragua, and Mexico.

The South Texas Sightings

The more recent sightings, dating to south Texas in 2004, have the telltale exsanguination signature, but the description of the animal is completely different than the reports coming out of Puerto Rico.

This version of the Chupacabra is four legged, with hindquarters higher than the front legs. The appearance is basically canine, although the animal is hairless. The skin is a leathery, grayish blue and so tough it's likened to elephant hide.

The canine teeth are greatly elongated and the bony ridge on top of the skull called the sagittal crest is more

pronounced than in domestic dogs.
T
hanks to the fact that folks in Texas keep guns ever at the
ready, there is physical evidence of the existence of this
Chupacabra.

In 2005 in Elmendorff, Texas, rancher Devin McAnally
tallied four sighting of a strange dog-like creature stalking
his chickens. Although the animal was extremely wary,
McAnally was finally able to kill it. He kept the bones and
teeth of what he believes was a Chupacabra.

Also in 2005 in Pollok, Texas, Ben O'Quinn shot a supposed
Chupacabra after first sending his son Tyrel under the
porch to pull the live animal out after the family dogs
cornered it. (When it doubt, sacrifice the kids first.)

The animal they killed was also smokey gray, hairless, and
had over-sized teeth. Although they did not keep the
carcass, they did take detailed photographs of the creature's
crusty skin and big teeth that support the idea that
whatever these animals may be, they are suffering from
some kind of illness.

Chupacabra Forensics

In 2007, Phylis Canion, a rancher in Cuero, Texas lost a lot
of chickens to supposed Chupacabra attacks. She retrieved
the carcass of one of the creatures after it was hit by a car
and froze the head to preserve the biological evidence. She
also saw the animal skulking around her ranch and on at
least one occasion it ran in front of her car.

Hair and skin samples from the Elmendorff and Cuero Chupacabras were examined and DNA testing was conducted. The conclusions were consistent with some type of canine species.

Veterinary pathologists at Texas A&M University theorized that what these South Texas ranchers killed was some sort of wolf / coyote hybrid and said they believed the animals were suffering from severe skin conditions, perhaps some variant of mange.

Similar testing was conducted on hair samples removed from a supposed Chupacabra nest in Puerto Rico that also came back as canine, debunking the theory that what witnesses were really seeing were rhesus monkeys.

Although the monkeys are not indigenous to Puerto Rico, there is an established population descended from animals that escaped from research laboratories.

Canion subsequently found a second suspected Chupacabra on a neighboring ranch. When a veterinary pathologist examined this animal's skin, the conclusion was that the animal was definitely a carnivore.

What is more interesting, since a lot of dead chickens would testify the Chupacabra is a meat eater, is that the vet said the animal had, at one time, been covered with a full coat of hair. This finding further supports the theory of an extreme skin condition accounting for the bizarre blue-gray color and leathery texture of the hide.

DNA testing on this second Cuero animal also showed that on the female parental side it was a coyote, and on the male side wolf. Even in the face of that kind of scientific evidence, however, witnesses in the area insist they know what a mangey coyote looks like and these critters are something else altogether.

Uh. Yeah. Folks? Pick up a dictionary. See the definition of "hybrid."

Even though the Chupacabra story has been blown completely out of proportion thanks to the Internet and popular culture, it's one of my favorite cryptids because of the evidence collected in South Texas. I think what the ranchers down there were (and maybe are still) seeing will turn out to be an instance of an accidental genetic cross gone horribly wrong.

Maybe the offspring of this hybridization were in so much discomfort from their congenital skin condition that they became unusually aggressive. Maybe they weren't strong enough to do more than lick the blood out of their kills, thus the exsanguination.

I don't know for sure. But the DNA finding of a hybrid animal is a whole lot more than investigators usually get in one of these cases. Now, as for what was or wasn't seen in Puerto Rico and why the descriptions were so different than the Texas "Chupacabras?" For that I have no answers and neither do cryptozoologists.

The Michigan Dogman

Like the Chupacabra straying over into the area of alien livestock mutilations, various types of "dog men" or outright "werewolves" are definitely straddling the cryptozoological / paranormal boundary line.

If we go with the first interpretation, we're discussing some kind of human / wolf hybrid. Door number two takes us into humans who can assume another shape either as a consequence of a curse / infection or because they're shapeshifters (which is the Native American take on the beasts.)

The one I want to look at is the Michigan Dogman, which is popularly believed to be a werewolf. The origin of the legend goes back as far as 1887 in Wexford County, Michigan, but this cryptid literally hit the charts when Steve Cook, a DJ at WTCM-FM in Traverse City wrote and recorded a song about the Dogman, which he played as an April Fool's Day joke in 1987.

Just a word to the wise. Be wary of playing jokes that involve cryptids. True believers will come out of the woodwork, which is exactly what happened in this case. Now, to give Cook credit, he sold cassette recordings of the song and donated the money to an animal shelter, so he gets Brownie points for that.

Cook wound up being regarded as a local expert on the Dogman, and over the years collected hundreds of reports of sightings and -- of course -- he built a website. Let's just set Cook aside for a second and consider what people thought they were seeing.

Reported Dogman Sightings

Residents in the area around the Huron-Mantisee National Forest have report strange howling noises for years, often in close proximity to farmhouses. The sound is a combination of both a wolf howl and a scream. Often eyewitnesses smell something horrible and see a pair of red eyes in the darkness.

Bigfoot isn't the only one! There are sightings throughout the American Mid-West of various "dog men" including the Beast of Bray Road and the Michigan Dogman.

People who have actually encountered the creature say that it stands on its hind legs at a height of about 7 feet / 2.13

meters. The face is wolf-like with an extended muzzle and the ears are tall and pointed.

As an example, in 1979, a bow hunter was out in a remote area near the forest. At dusk, he heard noises of something following him. When he moved, it moved. He got out of there as fast as he could, but went back the next day and found large footprints in the mud with at least three claws visible.

He made casts and took the prints to the Michigan Department of Natural Resources. The game biologists there could not say for sure what the man had encountered.

Subsequently, however, experts have looked at the casts and determined they are canine, but speculate that the size is greatly distorted due to the expansion of the mud when the animal's body weight pushed it outward with each step.

The Gable Film Hoax

Okay, so fast-forward to March 2010 when the Dogman was featured in an episode of *MonsterQuest*. As part of the analysis of Cook's evidence, the show took a closer look at a film he claimed to have received in the mail in 2006.

(Even though *MonsterQuest* is getting a little dated, some of the episodes are worth a look. Ditto for *Destination Truth*. I wouldn't take either as cryptid gospel, but it's entertaining streaming fare if you're bored on a Saturday afternoon and it'll get you asking questions.)

By 2007, the Dogman footage was all over the Internet, and a second film later surfaced theoretically showing the aftermath of the events in the initial footage. That's when eyebrows really went up. The timing of the release was suspicious and in theory the second film showed a police investigation complete with the mangled (read "torn in two") body of the victim.

But, that's getting ahead of ourselves. Back to the original story. Cook said a woman mailed a roll of 8mm film to him that she accidentally purchased in a box of junk she bought as a complete lot an an estate sale. There was a paper tag on the box that said "Gable Case," so the roll became known as the "Gable Film."

The footage appeared to have been shot in the 1970s. In the final frames of the film, an unknown creature is seen to the right of the frame in an area of sparse cover. The animal moves back and forth to the left and right with a rolling, jumping motion and then charges the camera.

When closely examined, the end of the film actually shows teeth grasping the camera, and in some of the frames, the reflection of a young man can be seen taking the video. Wildlife experts who looked at the frames said the creature was more ape-like than canine, and actually resembled a gorilla.

Film experts immediately saw a lot of indication that the whole thing was a hoax and, after a year of investigation, Cook admitted that it was bogus.

The filmmaker, said he made the movie in an effort to keep the excitement over the Dogman myth going. He went to Cook who posted the footage knowing it was fake. Whether these jokers meant any harm or not, a hoax is still a hoax.

The *MonsterQuest* people said they "uncovered" the fake, Cook and the guy who made the film said they told the producers from the start that it was a fake and they included the so-called "investigation" to make the episode more dramatic.

The problem now is the same one that follows every other really good hoax. Anyone who does see something in and around the Huron-Mantisee National Forest now has to overcome the additional layer of skepticism generated by these fakers.

That's not right. I refer you to the case of the Winkelmanns and the Jersey Devil. Polygraph tests showed that these people are honestly convinced they saw something that night they can't explain.

They're not lying, and they want to know what, if anything is really out there. Liars who fabricate evidence get in the way of that and make all people genuinely interested in investigating cryptids look nuts, which they're not.

Chapter 6 – Flying Cryptids

A few years back I was out hiking when I was practically strafed by a Red-Tailed Hawk. Dang thing nearly took my head off, but it wasn't interested in me. The target was a squirrel that never had a chance.

As I stood there watching the hawk fly off with that squirrel dangling from its talons, I remember thinking how glad I was that nothing was going to come swooping down to snatch me up.

Which is exactly why flying cryptids are so danged scary. What could be more horrible than something that can lift a human off the ground and carry them away for lunch?

The Jersey Devil

The Jersey Devil is reputed to be one of these bizarre flying monsters. It's believed to live deep in the Pine Barrens, more than one million acres of forest land sitting between Philadelphia on the southwest and New York City on the northeast.

The creature, which seems to have no fear of humans, is described in a variety of ways. The body is basically similar to that of a horse or a deer (size estimates vary), but the creature has the wings of a bat. The feet are hoofed, much like a goat, and the tail is long and serpentine.

Depending on the eyewitness in question, some people say the overall look is monkey-like (or gargoyle-like), while other says the Jersey Devil is more of a winged dog. In keeping with the origin story I'm about to tell, you get a definite "demon" vibe with this thing.

All the witnesses agree, however, that the creature is dark, grotesque, and can let out a scream that will stop your blood cold in your veins. People who have come face to face with what they believe to be the Jersey Devil have been terrified out of their minds.

The Leeds Family

There's a pretty spooky origin myth for this cryptid, and one that suggests when a woman has had enough, seriously bad things can happen. (Since I have three ex-wives, I can attest to this fact personally.)

In 1735, Jane Leeds and her husband Daniel lived in a cabin lying within the Pine Barrens. Locals described the family, which included 12 children, as somewhat strange.

When Jane was pregnant with Number 13, and no doubt sick unto death of motherhood, she supposedly asked God to make this child a devil. (We are assuming to discourage Daniel from exercising his marital privileges.)

Everything went fine with the delivery, and the kid popped out just as normal as you please – blond, blue-eyed, perfect in every way. Then, however, a horrible and rapid transformation took place.

The child grew into a huge monster with the head of a

horse, glowing red eyes, a set of horns, bat wings, and a serpent's tail. It let out a scream as its horrified mother looked on, and then escaped up the chimney.

Since that time, the Jersey Devil is said to have terrorized the region, and it is true that a large number of sightings are made within a 30 mile / 48.28 km radius of the original site of the Leeds' cabin.

What makes this case so interesting is that the people seeing the Jersey Devil are not the gimme-cap-wearing, trailer-park-dwelling variety of eyewitnesses so frequently associated with cryptid sightings.

Now, lest I be mistaken for an elitist bastard, I own many gimme caps and have no problem with trailer dwelling. I do, however, have a problem with eyewitness accounts that start with, "Me and my buddy Luther were sitting outside the doublewide plowing through a 12-pack of Bud when we seen . . ."

At any rate, at one time or another, police officers, postmasters, elected officials, and business people have seen the Jersey Devil. The creature is also supposed to be a precursor of war, with recorded sightings before the Civil War, Spanish American War, World War I, and World War II, and the Vietnam War. (Apparently the Devil understood that Korea was just a "police action.")

The "classic" Jersey Devil sightings date from a week in 1909 when the winged monster supposedly covered vast tracks of land all over southern New Jersey, parts of New

York, and Pennsylvania. (With record speed, I might add, and covering distances a jet might have trouble with today.)

Sightings in 1909

In 1909 over a one-week period that began on January 16, there were more than fifty sightings of the Jersey Devil. The events touched off near panic in the state, since the beast was seen by whole groups of people and various leading citizens.

During the week, police officers saw the thing three times, and one officer, James Sackville, actually took a shot at it. A group of firemen claimed to have blasted the Devil off a rooftop with a stream of water from their hose while employees with the telegraph company insisted they shot the thing in the wing.

Tracks were found all over southern New Jersey, where people feared for their lives. Locals formed posses and headed out to kill the monster a la the mob at the base of Frankenstein's castle.

In Burlington, New Jersey virtually every yard boasted a set of unexplained tracks. Some of the prints went up to trees and disappeared, others stopped in the middle of the road or fields suggesting the thing took off flying. Sets of tracks also appeared to skip from one roof to the next.

On January 19th the Jersey Devil woke up Mr. and Mrs. Nelson Evans of Gloucester and hung around outside their bedroom window for ten minutes at approximately 2 a.m.

In Clementon, a whole trolley full of people saw something circling in the sky overhead, and in Trenton a city councilman heard flapping wings and found tracks in his yard.

One thing's for certain. The degree of panic was good for the area churches. People packed the pews begging God to protect them, convinced that there was indeed a devil loose among them.

So far as I can make out, the Jersey Devil has never actually killed a person, nor does it seem to be particularly interested in carrying people off anywhere, including the fires of hell.

The Devil has been linked to livestock deaths in the region for decades, with chickens taking the biggest hit. (In 1966, however, the thing supposedly raided a farm and plowed through 31 ducks, 3 geese, 4 cats, and 2 dogs.)

> ***Common Factoid***: Cryptids are hell on chickens. Chupacabras in particular are hell on chickens *and* goats. Apparently, cows go down most often to aliens. But chickens? They not only get eaten by cryptids, they get used routinely as cryptid *bait*.

The Winkelmann Sighting

In January 2004, Laurie Winkelmann and her son saw the Jersey Devil in their backyard in Wharton State Park in the Pine Barrens.

The sighting happened at night. The Winkelmanns had been outside enjoying a snowstorm. They headed in for dinner, but forgot to turn off the Christmas lights in the yard.

Laurie asked her son, then 11 years of age, to accompany her back outside. When they reached the lights, which were strung across the backyard, the boy looked up into the trees and froze.

There, above their heads, was a giant black creature looking at them. Without warning, the thing swooped toward the pair.

Laurie, in a panic, grabbed her son and began dragging him toward the house. The beast flew over their heads and landed on the roof, directly above the door for which they were heading.

As Laurie approached the door, she could hear the creature on the roof moving down toward them. She pushed her son inside and slammed the door.

The next morning, Laurie's husband found tracks on the roof, which he photographed. When a local hunter could not identify what kind of animal made the prints, Winkelmann took the pictures to the Parks and Recreation Department for examination. Again, no definitive conclusion could be drawn.

The tracks on the roof were 9 inches / 22.86 cm x 5 inches / 12.7 cm and distributed 4 feet / 1.22 meters apart. Whatever had made them appeared to have walked on two legs. Through the years, the Winkelmanns have been incredibly consistent in relating the details of this sighting. There are, however, a number of problems with the evidence in this case.

The photographs that are the only existing record of the tracks are taken at a low angle, making positive identification and real analysis problematic. Arguably, the slant of the perspective could make the prints look bigger than they actually were. Also, animal tracks in snow deteriorate and distort rapidly.

It has been suggested that the Winkelmanns actually had an encounter with a large Great Horned Owl that swooped down over them and perched on the roof. The owl then hopped toward them, thus giving the impression that it walked on two legs.

Laurie and her son refuse to have any part of that explanation. Both insist that the story they have told repeatedly is the truth, and both passed polygraph tests that verified the mother and son absolutely believe they saw a huge winged creature in their backyard.

The Montauk Monster

In July 2008, Christina Pampalone photographed an odd creature that washed up on shore in Montauk, New York some 175 miles northeast of the Pine Barrens. The pictures ignited a storm of controversy that the thing lying on the beach might actually be a Jersey Devil.

Pampalone only released the photographs after another set of images appeared taken by another person who had been on the beach that day. Pampalone thought her pictures were better.

She speculated that the carcass was some kind of rodent, but many people immediately said the creature was tied to experiments being conducted at the Plum Island Animal Disease Center 18 miles away.

The rumors became so severe that the Plum Island officials actually commented on the authenticity of what was, by then, being referred to as the Montauk Monster.

Contrary to popular rumor, there has been no work of a military nature on Plum Island since the 1950s. The work that is done there is with livestock, and officials insist they are not a part of any biological weapons programs.

They say that what Pampalone photographed on the beach was likely a Boxer of a Bulldog that had been in the ocean long enough for the skin to slough off. The creature's "horned snout," is simply the nasal portion of the dog's skull that has been exposed, and the pronounced lower jaw is typical in such breeds.

Beyond all that, the Montauk Monster, though interesting in its own right, didn't match any descriptions of the Jersey Devil and there was no evidence of wings. So are there any real animals that *could* be the Jersey Devil?

The Hammerhead Bat of Africa has been suggested as one candidate. They're large, with a wingspan of up to 3 feet / 0.9 meters and a lifespan of as much as 30 years.

This theory suggests the bats could have come over on slave ships in the 19th century and become established in the area. The problem with that, however, is that the New England is too cold for the tropical bats to survive.

Activity Has Declined in Recent Years

In recent years, sightings of the Jersey Devil have declined. Some experts theorize that as more civilization has pressed against the Pine Barrens, the creature has retreated far into the interior.

But, every time the idea starts floating around that the Jersey Devil is gone or that he's dead, the thing crops up again. Never get complacent around cryptids.
If this is indeed the devil spawn of Jane and Daniel Leeds,

their bouncing demonic boy child is now 280 years old and he's still got some Mommy issues. I'm just saying.

Giant Thunderbird

Depending on where you're located, giant flying creatures of this type are either called Rocs (in Europe) or Thunderbirds in America.

This is another cryptid that crosses the myth / reality boundary in specific ways. If you go study Native American spirituality, Thunderbirds have a whole different meaning and I'm not qualified to talk about that.

What people think they're seeing is yet another "surviving dinosaur" type cryptid, generally linked to one or another of the creatures classed as Pteranodons. You know, those winged things that are pretty much in every dinosaur movie ever made?

Pteranodons were, without a doubt, big flying reptiles with a wingspan of better than 20 feet / 6 meters. They called North America home. Fossils have been found in Alabama, Nebraska, Wyoming, Kansas, and South Dakota. They lived about 4 million years ago.

Pteranodons in the Old West

The origin story on the Thunderbird myth goes back to April 1890. A couple of cowboys out in Arizona are supposed to have killed a big bird-like creature. They described a featherless animal with smooth skin, huge wings, and the head of an alligator.

They took the thing into town where it was photographed on the side of a barn with the wings pinned out to their full width. Problem is, the picture has never been seen again, not even a copy.

The Illinois Sightings

In 1948 there was a sighting in Overland, Illinois when three people saw what they thought was a plane passing overhead – until the plane flapped its wings. A few weeks later, a man and his son had a similar experience in Alton, Illinois.

Things died down until July 25, 1977 when three boys playing ball in a back yard were chased by two large, unidentified birds. Two of the kids got away, but the third one was lifted a couple of feet off the ground and carried a few yards until he managed to get loose.

The boy who was attacked, Marlon Lowe, was ten years old. His mother witnessed her son being carried along for about 40 feet / 12.2 meters at a height of about 3 feet / 0.9

meters. Her screams apparently caused the bird to drop her son. The birds flew away without trying to recapture their "prey."

The boy, although scared half out of his mind, was only scratched up. At least five adults saw the birds and said they were black with white bands around the neck. The creatures had beaks that were long and curved. The eyewitnesses estimated the birds' wingspan to be at least 10 feet / 3.05 meters.

Three days later a similar bird was spotted flying over a nearby farm. A group was flying radio controlled airplanes nearby, which provided perspective against which to measure the flying animals. These witnesses also believed they were seeing something with a 10-foot / 3.05-meter wingspan.

There were also sightings on July 28 and July 30, the latter yielding 100 feet of film. The Illinois Department of Conservation dismissed the two birds in the film as Turkey Vultures, but wildlife experts said the animals were too big.

The biggest bird in the United States is the California Condor with a wingspan of 9 feet / 2.7 meters, but it's not too likely those big boys took a vacation to Illinois just to mess with the locals.

The Andean Condor has been suggested as a likely culprit since they're black and have a ring around their necks, and the wingspan is right. Trouble is, they don't have the strength to pick up a 10-year-old kid and carry him 40 feet.

More Recent Sightings

In October 2002, there were a series of sightings in southwest Alaska. This time witnesses described a creature that seemed to be straight out of *Jurassic Park*, (thank you Stephen Spielberg for the now de facto cultural reference base.) The wingspan of the animal was reported to be 14 feet / 4.3 meters

Reports surfaced in San Antonio, Texas in 2007 (of an incident that actually occurred in 1997) and in Las Cruces, New Mexico (of a 1998 sighting.) In these cases both of the creatures were said to have a wingspan of as much as 20 feet / 6.09 meters.

Ornithologists say that the Thunderbird myth is impossible for one simple reason – there's not enough food out there for birds of this reported size to survive. Also, bird watching is an enormously popular pastime. There are folks all over the place out there with binoculars and none of them are reporting giant flying prehistoric Tweetie birds.

The problem of perspective with a flying object is pretty much the same as something swimming. If you don't have a point of comparison, and you're excited and the adrenaline is flowing, stuff starts looking a whole lot bigger than it really is.

Again, I think the *Jurassic Park* effect is kicking in here. We *want* some of the dinosaurs to have survived, even though the idea that they might have is enough to scare the holy living crud out of us. Man vs. dinosaur is not an equation for survival, but the idea is definitely exciting.

Other Flying Cryptids {h2}

Certainly the Jersey Devil and the Thunderbird are not the only unknowns in the genre of flying crypids. There are several creatures around the world described as left-over dinosaurs, great big ole bats, giant birds, or some combination thereof. Some examples include:

- The **Ahool** is a flying bat-like creature in the deep rainforest regions of Java named for its call, which sounds like "ahoooool." The thing is supposed to have a 10-foot / 3 meter wingspan and its body is roughly the size of a human infant and covered in gray fur. The eyes are large and dark and the forearms are outfitted with big claws.

- There's also a supposed cryptid bat in Central Africa called the **Olitiau**, which has a 6-12 foot / 2-4 meter wingspan. The creature's body is black with red or dark brown wings and in a nice grisly touch, the lower jaw is studded with 2-in / 50 mm serrated teeth.

- The **Kongamato** has been spotted in the Congo, Angola, and Western Zambia although it's never been photographed. The bulk of the evidence for the existence of this creature, which is supposed to be a surviving pterorsaur (another prehistoric flying reptile), comes from eyewitness accounts. The animals apparently live along rivers and have a propensity for attacking small boats. Descriptions place the wingspan at 4-7 feet / 1.2-2.1 meters. The overall look is a "prehistoric" body that, depending on the account is either red or black.

- On the Indonesian island of Seram, the **Orang-bati** appears to be a cross between a bat cryptid and a pterorsaur, but with kind of a monkey-like face. This once snatches children and carries them off to eat them at its home base on Mount Kairatu.

- The **Mothman** is a relatively well known cryptid after a rash of sightings in the area around Point Pleasant, West Virginia from November 15, 1966 to November 15, 1967. In 1975 a book by John Keel, *The*

Mothman Prophecies, also popularized the creature, which is described as standing 7 feet / 2.13 meters in height with huge wings and, of course, red eyes.

- The **Owlman of Mawnan** or the Cornish Owlman is the English equivalent of the Mothman. This beast was first sighted hovering above the Mawnan church tower by two sisters, ages 9 and 12, in April 1976. Two months later, a pair of teenage girls on a camping trip saw an owl as large as a man with red eyes and pointed ears. It was seen again in June and August of 1978, with subsequent encounters in 1989 and 1995.

For the record, the largest flying bird found in fossil form in 1983 is a giant seabird that lived off the coast of South Carolina 25-28 million years ago. *Pelagornis sandersi* had a 20-24 foot / 6.1-7.3 meter wingspan. It fed on fish and squid near the water's surface.

Chapter 7 – So You Want to Hunt Cryptids?

So, you've read all this and you've decided you want to be a cryptid hunter. Obviously it helps if you actually live somewhere with suspected cryptid activity.

It's not out of the realm of possibility, however, that you could jump on a plane or drive somewhere just to have a monster-hunting vacation. Heck, birdwatchers do it all the time – and for that matter, so do Bigfoot hunters.

No Trespassing

Once you're on the ground or out on the water looking for something, there's one really serious ground rule: Do *NOT* trespass on someone's land.

If you can't access public land to look for any sort of critter and you want to be in a specific area *ASK THE LANDOWNER.*

If you're told no, pull up your panties and deal. Going over somebody's fence line is not cool and in some places can get you shot.

Don't Shoot at Everything That Moves

Second, if you are going against something that can hurt you and you are *PROFICIENT* with firearms as in *LICENSED* and / or *TRAINED*, it's fine to carry a gun, but don't be a bonehead and try to shoot everything that moves.

Get Photographic Evidence

If at all possible, try to get photographic evidence, *NOT* a carcass. These things are rare, they're out there for the most part minding their own business, and they don't deserve to be blasted for the hell of it.

Invest in a good-quality super-zoom camera — not the camera in your smartphone —and learn how to use it. Take extra batteries and try to get good images, and/or video.

I also recommend a lightweight, but high-powered set of binoculars. The Bushnell Legend Ultra HDs are 10 x 42 mm. They'll set you back a couple of hundred bucks, but they are totally worth it.

The Bushnells have superb low-light capability, which you'll need since a lot of animals are most active at dusk and dawn. These binoculars also have an ultra-wide field of view, and they're water and fog proof.

Keep Your Original Images in Untouched Condition

ALWAYS keep the *ORIGINAL* file of all digital images. Only crop or sharpen a copy. You will be accused of being a faker and you need to be able to produce an original, out-of-the-camera, untouched version of your image.

Geotag Your Location

Carry a GPS and geotag the exact location of the sighting. Trust me, skeptics will try to verify any really outstanding evidence you find and it's to everyone's advantage that you supply as much information as possible to help them do that.

Remember the Mansi picture of Champ that looks so great? Yeah. No negatives and the folks who shot the image could never find the spot again. And they wonder why their claims were met with skepticism?

Afterword

Look, I told you from the start, this is an armchair hobby for me. It's fun to keep up with the latest sightings online and I like to watch documentaries and cheesy monster hunting shows. (And yes, I watched *Ghost Hunters*, too.)

I've written about survival topics before that involve variations on the undead apocalypse, so clearly I'm a believer. You may think I'm a believer smoking some good stuff, but you paddle your canoe and I'll paddle mine.

There are lots of things in the world we can't explain, and lots of things we just flat don't want to admit are really out there. Admitting that they're out there equals admitting our own vulnerability to being something's lunch, and most of us just can't go there.

The whole idea with this book was for me to share some stories with you about various kinds of cryptids that I find especially interesting. Lake monsters and sea monsters are in the mix because natural bodies of water are good hiding places for unknown creatures.

All the kinds of alleged hominids fascinate me, not just Bigfoot, but of course he is the king of this genre. Again, with the bulk of the sightings in the Pacific Northwest, that's prime country for something to be hiding.

As for the rest? The dog-like creatures? The chupacabara? The Jersey Devil? The Thunderbirds? I figure that's 50/50 proposition. I'm pretty sure the Jersey Devil is just folks being scared of the woods at night. I really do think the Thunderbird thing is a case of mistaken identity. Of them all? My money is on the chupacabra as panning out to be some kind of hybrid.

And werewolves or some variation there of? That's a topic for another day.

Relevant Websites

Above Top Secret
www.abovetopsecret.com

American Monsters
www.americanmonsters.com

Bigfoot Evidence
bigfootevidence.blogspot.com

Bigfoot Field Researchers Organization
www.bfro.net

British Columbia Scientific Cryptozoology Club
www.bcscc.ca

Champ Monster
www.champmonster.com

The Committee for Skeptical Inquiry
www.csicop.org

CryptoMundo
www.cryptomundo.com

Cryptid Wiki
cryptidz.wikia.com

Cryptozoology
Cryptozoology.com

The Cryptozoologist
www.lorencoleman.com

Cryptozoology Museum
www.cryptozoologymuseum.com

Cryptozoology News.com
www.cryptozoologynews.com

The Cryptic Zoo
www.newanimal.org

CryptoZooNews
www.cryptozoonews.com

Deep Sea News
www.deepseanews.com

The Florida Skunk Ape
www.floridaskunkape.com

Fouke Monster: The Beast and the Legend of Boggy Creek
www.foukemonster.net

The Legend of Michigan's Dogman
www.michigan-dogman.com

The Legend of Nessie: The Ultimate Loch Ness Monster Site
www.nessie.co.uk

Live Science
www.livescience.com

Ogopogo Quest
www.ogopogoquest.com

Paranormal Encyclopedia
www.paranormal-encyclopedia.com

Pre-Historic Wildlife
www.prehistoricwildlife.com

The Shadowlands
www.theshadowlands.net

The Skeptic's Dictionary
www.skepdic.com

Strange Mag
www.strangemag.com

Top Secret Writers
www.topsecretwriters.com

Unexplained Mysteries
www.unexplainedmysteries.com

Unknown Explorers
www.unknownexplorers.com

The UnMuseum
www.unmuseum.org

Weird U.S.
www.weirdus.com

The Werewolf Page
www.werewolfpage.com

For Further Reading

Yeah. Shock of shocks, people. There's A LOT of research being done in this field. Here's a sampling of articles and books just from 2000-2015. If you want to be a serious student of cryptozoology, there's nothing holding you back from doing that.

Armstrong, Philip. "Moa Citings." *The Journal of Commonwealth Literature* 45, no. 3 (2010): 325–39.

Aseer Manual, Chìppu Shakir and Joseph Selvin and Balu Saharathnam. "Mokele-Mbembe:" A Cryptozoological Animal of Centre African Prefecture: Veracity or Hoax." *World Applied Sciences Journal* 10, no. 5 (2010): 544–51.

Baker, Joseph O. and Scott Draper. "Diverse Supernatural Portfolios: Certitude, Exclusivity, and the Curvilinear Relationship Between Religiosity and Paranormal Beliefs." *Journal for the Scientific Study of Religion* 49, no. 3 (2010): 413–24.

Bartholomew, Robert E. "New Information Surfaces on World's Best Lake Monster Photo, Raising Questions." *Skeptical Inquirer* (2013):

Bayanov, Dmitri. "Historical Evidence for the Existence of Relict Hominoids."

Bindernagel, John and Jeff Meldrum. "Misunderstandings Arising From Treating the Sasquatch as a Subject of Cryptozoology."

Blake, Max, Darren Naish, Greger Larson, Charlotte L King, Geoff Nowell, Manabu Sakamoto, and Ross Barnett. "Multidisciplinary Investigation of a British Big Cat: A Lynx Killed in Southern England C. 1903." *Historical Biology* 26, no. 4 (2014): 441–48.

Brysse, Keynyn. "Cryptozoology, Archaeology and Palaeontology: Histories Near the High Table." *Annals of Science* 67, no. 4 (2010): 569–75.

Budd, Deena West. *The Weiser Field Guide to Cryptozoology: Werewolves, Dragons, Skyfish, Lizard Men, and Other Fascinating Creatures Real and Mysterious*. Weiser Books, 2010.

Carroll, Robert. *The Skeptic's Dictionary: A Collection of Strange Beliefs, Amusing Deceptions, and Dangerous Delusions*. John Wiley & Sons, 2011.

Childress, David Hatcher. *Yetis, Sasquatch & Hairy Giants*. Scb Distributors, 2010.

Coleman, Loren. "The Meaning of Cryptozoology." (2012):

Cressey, Daniel. "Cryptozoology: Beastly Fakes." *Nature* 499, no. 7459 (2013): 406–406.

Davis, Graeme. *Werewolves: A Hunter's Guide*. Osprey Publishing, 2015.

de Blécourt, Willem. "Monstrous Theories: Werewolves and the Abuse of History." *Preternature: Critical and*

Historical Studies on the Preternatural 2, no. 2 (2013): 188–212.

De Vos, Gail. *What Happens Next? Contemporary Urban Legends and Popular Culture.* ABC-CLIO, 2012.

Dennett, Michael. "Science and Footprints." *Skeptical Inquirer* (2013):

Enenkel, Karl AE. "The Species and Beyond: Classification and the Place of Hybrids in Early Modern Zoology." *Zoology in Early Modern Culture: Intersections of Science, Theology, Philology, and Political and Religious Education* 32 (2014): 57.

Fanthorpe, Lionel and Patricia Fanthorpe. *The Big Book of Mysteries.* Dundurn, 2010.

Flitcroft, Jean. *The Cryptid Files: Loch Ness.* Little Island, 2010.

Godfrey, Linda S. *Real Wolfmen: True Encounters in Modern America.* Penguin, 2012.

Goulden, Murray. "Hobbits, Hunters and Hydrology: Images of a "missing Link," and Its Scientific Communication." *Public Understanding of Science* (2011): 0963662511419627.

Guiley, Rosemary Ellen. *Monsters of West Virginia: Mysterious Creatures in the Mountain State.* Stackpole Books, 2014.

Hairr, John. *Monsters of North Carolina: Mysterious Creatures in the Tar Heel State*. Stackpole Books, 2013.

Harrison, Guy P. *50 Popular Beliefs That People Think Are True*. Prometheus Books, 2012.

Hawkeswood, Trevor J. *Light and Dark: My Experiences With the Paranormal*. Balboa Press, 2013.

Hill, Sharon. "Amateur Paranormal Research and Investigation Groups Doing Sciency Things."

Hill, Sharon. "Cryptozoology and Pseudoscience." *Skeptical Inquirer* 21, no. 3 (2011):

Jenkins, Greg. *Chronicles of the Strange and Uncanny in Florida*. Pineapple Press Inc, 2010.

Jobling, Mark A. "The Truth is Out There." *Investigative Genetics* 4 (2013): 24.

Knott, Dana and Kristine Szabo. "Bigfoot Hunting Academic Library Outreach to Elementary School Students." *College & Research Libraries News* 74, no. 7 (2013): 346–48.

Lang, Le Duing, Nathalie Tessier, Marc Gauthier, Renee Wissink, Hélène Jolicoeur, and François-Joseph Lapointe. "Genetic Confirmation of Cougars (Puma Concolor) in Eastern Canada." *Northeastern Naturalist* 20, no. 3 (2013): 383–96.

Laycock, Joseph P. "Approaching the Paranormal." *Nova Religio: The Journal of Alternative and Emergent Religions* 18, no. 1 (2014): 5–15.

Loxton, Daniel and Donald R Prothero. *Abominable Science: Origins of the Yeti, Nessie, and Other Famous Cryptids.* Columbia University Press, 2013.

Mackenzie, Louisa. "French Early Modern Sea-Monsters and Modern Identities, Via Bruno Latour." *Animals and Early Modern Identity* (2014): 329.

Marshall, Michael. "Lost Treasures: The Sea-Monster Seal." *New Scientist* 213, no. 2850 (2012): 44.

Mayo, Matthew P. *Myths and Mysteries of New Hampshire: True Stories of the Unsolved and Unexplained.* Globe Pequot, 2014.

McClure, Randall, Rachel Cooke, and Anna Carlin. "The Search for the Skunk Ape: Studying the Impact of an Online Information Literacy Tutorial on Student Writing." *Journal of information literacy* 5, no. 2 (2011): 26–45.

McCormick, Charlie T and Kim Kennedy White. *Folklore: An Encyclopedia of Beliefs, Customs, Tales, Music, and Art.* ABC-CLIO, 2011.

Meldrum, Jeff and Zhou Guoxing. "Footprint Evidence of the Chinese Yeren." American Journal of Physical Anthropology 144 (2011): 213–213.

Miller, Julie and Grant Osborn. *Something is Out There: Unlocking Australia's Paranormal Secrets*. Allen & Unwin, 2010.

Naish, D. "A Sea Monster Poster for the 9th European Symposium of Cryptozoology." *Tetrapod Zoology blog* (2010):

Normandin, Sebastian. "Regal, Searching for Sasquatch: Crackpots, Eggheads, and Cryptozoology. Basingstoke: Palgrave Macmillan, 2011. Pp. Xi+ 249. Isbn 978-0-2300-11147-9.£ 55.00 (Hardback)." *The British Journal for the History of Science* 45, no. 04 (2012): 699–700.

Paulsen, Gary. *The Creature of Black Water Lake: World of Adventure Series*. Yearling, 2011.

Pooley, William G. "Monsters of the Gévaudan: The Making of a Beast." *Western Folklore* 71, no. 1 (2012): 73.

Pye, Michael and Kirsten Dalley. *Lost Cities and Forgotten Civilizations*. The Rosen Publishing Group, 2013.

Radford, Benjamin. *Tracking the Chupacabra: The Vampire Beast in Fact, Fiction, and Folklore*. UNM Press, 2011.

Radford, Benjamin. "Bigfoot At 50." *Pseudoscience and Deception: The Smoke and Mirrors of Paranormal Claims* (2013): 161.

Radford, Benjamin. *Mysterious New Mexico: Miracles, Magic, and Monsters in the Land of Enchantment*. UNM Press, 2014.

Redfern, Nick. *True Stories of Real-Life Monsters*. The Rosen Publishing Group, 2014.

Regal, Brian. *Searching for Sasquatch: Crackpots, Eggheads, and Cryptozoology*. Palgrave Macmillan, 2011.

Revai, Cheri and Cheri Farnsworth. *Haunted Massachusetts*. Stackpole Books, 2014.

Emmer, Rick. *Kraken: Fact or Fiction*. Infobase Publishing, 2010.

Emmer, Rick. *Loch Ness Monster: Fact or Fiction*. Infobase Publishing, 2010.

Ritvo, Harriet. "Brian Regal. Searching for Sasquatch: Crackpots, Eggheads, and Cryptozoology." *The American Historical Review* 120, no. 2 (2015): 586–87.

Ruickbie, Leo. *A Brief Guide to the Supernatural: Ghosts, Vampires and the Paranormal*. Hachette UK, 2012.

Schembri, Elise. "Cryptozoology as a Pseudoscience: Beasts in Transition." *Studies by Undergraduate Researchers at Guelph* 5, no. 1 (2011): 5–10.

Sharman, Paul. "Exmoor Dreaming." *Sacred Species and Sites: Advances in Biocultural Conservation* (2012): 111.

Sharps, Matthew J, Elaine Newborg, Stephanie Van Arsdall, Jordan DeRuiter, Bill Hayward, and Brianna Alcantar. "Paranormal Encounters as Eyewitness Phenomena:

Psychological Determinants of Atypical Perceptual Interpretations." *Current Psychology* 29, no. 4 (2010): 320–27.

Shermer, Michael and Bryan Farha. *Pseudoscience and Deception: The Smoke and Mirrors of Paranormal Claims*. University Press of America, 2013.

Shiel, Lisa A. *Top Secret Sasquatch: Exposing the True Nature of Bigfoot and Its Controversial Connections to UFOs, the Fossil Record, and Human History (Forbidden Bigfoot, Part Two)*. Jacobsville Books, 2012.

Shields, Sharma. "Field Guide to Monsters of the Inland Northwest." *The Kenyon Review* (2011): 112–24.

Smith, Jonathan C. *Pseudoscience and Extraordinary Claims of the Paranormal: A Critical Thinker's Toolkit*. John Wiley & Sons, 2011.

Souliere, Michelle. *Strange Maine: True Tales From the Pine Tree State*. The History Press, 2011.

Ståhlberg, Sabira and Ingvar Svanberg. "Wildmen in Central Asia." *Animals Out of Place: Cryptozoology in Anthropological Perspective* (2012):

Steiger, Brad. *Real Monsters, Gruesome Critters, and Beasts From the Darkside*. Visible Ink Press, 2010.

Streicher, Thomas James. *Extra-Planetary Experiences: Alien-Human Contact and the Expansion of Consciousness*. Inner Traditions/Bear & Co, 2012.

Sykes, Bryan C, Rhettman A Mullis, Christophe Hagenmuller, Terry W Melton, and Michel Sartori. "Genetic Analysis of Hair Samples Attributed to Yeti, Bigfoot and Other Anomalous Primates." *Proceedings of the Royal Society B: Biological Sciences* 281, no. 1789 (2014): 20140161.

Taylor, Emily K. "Skeptics and Believers: An Analysis of the Power of Local Legend," diss., Ball State University, 2011.

Trachtengerts, Michael. "The Large-Bodied Hominoids of the Himalayas." *Scientific Journal of Zoology* 1, no. 3 (2012): 52–60.

Walker, Anthony R. "Images of the Wildman in Southeast Asia: An Anthropological Perspective [Book Review]." (2010):

Whitcomb, Jonathan David and Paperback CreateSpace. *Live Pterosaurs in America.* CreateSpace, 2010.

Williams, William F. *Encyclopedia of Pseudoscience: From Alien Abductions to Zone Therapy.* Routledge, 2013.

Wilson, Patty A. *Monsters of Pennsylvania: Mysterious Creatures in the Keystone State.* Stackpole Books, 2010.

Wilson, Steve. "Folkloric Science." *New Scientist* 213, no. 2853 (2012): 36.

Woetzel, Dave and Richard Dobbs. *Chronicles of Dinosauria: The History & Mystery of Dinosaurs and Man.* New Leaf Publishing Group, 2013.

Wood, Scott. *London Urban Legends.* Best Books, 2013.

Woodley, MA, D Naish, and CA McCormick. "A Baby Sea-Serpent No More: Reinterpreting Hagelund's Juvenile" Cadborosaur" Report." *Journal of Scientific Exploration* 25, no. 3 (2011): 497.

Wright, E Lynne. *Myths and Mysteries of Florida: True Stories of the Unsolved and Unexplained.* Rowman & Littlefield, 2012.

Index

Feeding Baby
Cynthia Cherry
978-1941070000

Axolotl
Lolly Brown
978-0989658430

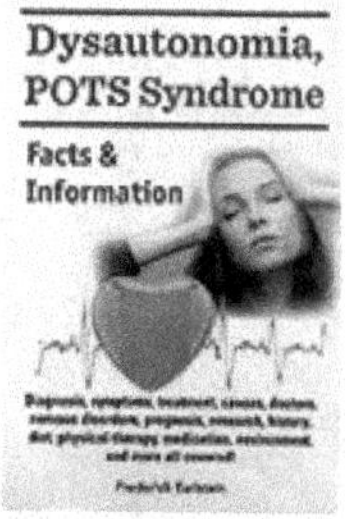

Dysautonomia, POTS
Syndrome
Frederick Earlstein
978-0989658485

Degenerative Disc
Disease Explained
Frederick Earlstein
978-0989658485

Sinusitis, Hay Fever,
Allergic Rhinitis Explained
Frederick Earlstein
978-1941070024

Wicca
Riley Star
978-1941070130

Zombie Apocalypse
Rex Cutty
978-1941070154

Capybara
Lolly Brown
978-1941070062

Eels As Pets
Lolly Brown
978-1941070167

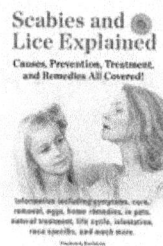

Scabies and Lice Explained
Frederick Earlstein
978-1941070017

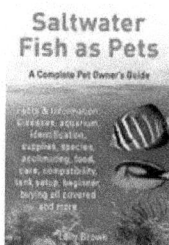

Saltwater Fish As Pets
Lolly Brown
978-0989658461

Torticollis Explained
Frederick Earlstein
978-1941070055

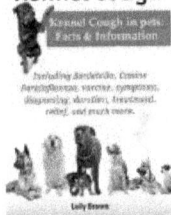

Kennel Cough
Lolly Brown
978-0989658409

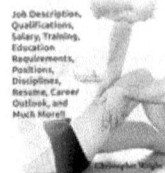

Physiotherapist, Physical
Therapist
Christopher Wright
978-0989658492

Rats, Mice, and Dormice
As Pets
Lolly Brown
978-1941070079

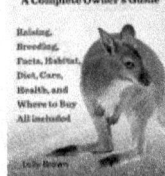

Wallaby and Wallaroo Care
Lolly Brown
978-1941070031

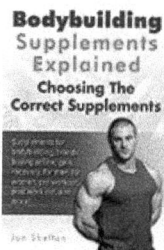

Bodybuilding Supplements
Explained
Jon Shelton
978-1941070239

Demonology
Riley Star
978-19401070314

Pigeon Racing
Lolly Brown
978-1941070307

www.ingramcontent.com/pod-product-compliance
Lightning Source LLC
Chambersburg PA
CBHW060909280326
41934CB00007B/1247